KU-694-659

The Foster Carer's Handbook on Parenting Teenagers

Henrietta Bond

700004303630

amBAAF
ADOPTION & FOSTERING ACADEMY

Published by
CoramBAAF Adoption and Fostering Academy
41 Brunswick Square
London WC1N 1AZ
www.corambaaf.org.uk

Coram Academy Limited, registered as a company limited by guarantee
in England and Wales number 9697712, part of the Coram group,
charity number 312278

© Henrietta Bond, 2019

British Library Cataloguing in Publication Data
A catalogue record for this book is available from the British Library

ISBN 978 1 910039 77 9

Project management by Jo Francis, Publications, CoramBAAF
Designed by Helen Joubert Design
Printed in Great Britain by The Lavenham Press

Trade distribution by Turnaround Publisher Services, Unit 3, Olympia
Trading Estate, Coburg Road, London N22 6TZ

All rights reserved. Apart from any fair dealing for the purposes of
research or private study, or criticism or review, as permitted under the
Copyright, Designs and Patents Act 1988, this publication may not be
reproduced, stored in a retrieval system, or transmitted in any form or by
any means, without the prior written permission of the publishers.

The moral right of the author has been asserted in accordance with the
Copyright, Designs and Patents Act 1988.

 For the latest news on CoramBAAF titles and special offers, sign up to
our free publications bulletin at https://corambaaf.org.uk/subscribe.

Contents

Acknowledgements

Many thanks to all those foster carers, social workers and young people who have helped me with the writing of this book. Without the experiences and insights you've shared with me over the years, none of this would be possible. I hope you know who you are! In particular, thanks to Sian Colley, a very experienced carer for young people who has shared so much of her wisdom and resourcefulness with me.

Sincere thanks also to Paul Adams at CoramBAAF for his support, generous sharing of knowledge and endless patience with my questions, and Katrina Wilson and Lisa Weintrobe, also at CoramBAAF, for being so helpful in so many ways.

Thanks also to Dyanna O'Brien, Phil and Jen Davey, and Fiona Darlington-Black for their help in reading and commenting on earlier versions of the manuscript.

Many thanks also to Jo Francis and Shaila Shah, at CoramBAAF, for all their work on this project.

About the author

Henrietta Bond is a writer, coach and communications consultant who has worked in the fields of adoption, fostering and leaving care for nearly 30 years. Previously BAAF's media and information officer, she became a freelance consultant and journalist, and worked on a variety of projects, including group wok with care-experienced children and young people. She has written a number of guides and her trilogy of novels for teenagers, the Control Freak series (available from CoramBAAF) came out of her close work with children and young people.

Henrietta is passionate about giving children and young people a voice and helping them to develop resilience and self-esteem, and is keen to develop the potential of coaching to help young people have more control over their own lives. As a writer, she also helps young people find creative ways to express themselves. Henrietta recognises that she has as much to learn from young people as they have to learn from her.

Introduction

Being a teenager isn't easy, and it's a miracle how anyone gets through the turbulence of those difficult years in one piece – and that applies to parents as much as to the young person! Deciding to foster someone else's teenagers is an amazing thing to do, and you need to get all of the information and support that you can, so you can fulfil this role to the very best of your ability.

You may have done a great job in raising your own teenagers, or you may have done an equally excellent job in raising fostered children already in your household. But once young people who have experienced abuse, neglect, loss and separation reach the adolescent years, the usual teenage problems may be magnified as the young person's changing brain reawakens many of the traumas and painful issues from their past. At the same time, their already fragmented sense of identity can become even more fragile, and they are exposed to impulsivity and powerfully confusing feelings, on top of all the problems they have already encountered.

It is a big challenge to rise to, but helping a teenager to negotiate this complex time in their life is an incredibly rewarding thing to do. You will probably come out of it feeling that you've learnt a great deal about the importance of resilience – both for yourself and for the young person – and while change certainly doesn't happen overnight, you will be able to help young people discover new and more effective ways of dealing with the challenges that life has thrown at them. You will also have the knowledge that you have given them the best possible chance to embark on adult life feeling that someone has valued them enough to see them through the ups and downs of this major period of transition.

Who is a teenager?

Tony Hipgrave (1989, p40) writes that adolescence is a:

...complex and largely artificial phenomenon. It begins with a biological change, puberty, and ends via a number of social definitions – for instance, leaving home, leaving school or college, or getting married...Broadly speaking, adolescence can be characterised as a period of continuing

protection from the full blast of the adult world, on condition that the individual adolescent will progressively display increasing responsibility and independence. On the face of it, and from the adult's perspective, this seems to be a sensible and caring sense of affairs, but it should not be forgotten that the adolescent may experience the teenage years as frustrating due to the excessive prohibition on them in respect of activities in which they clearly have the capacity to engage, particularly sexual activity and paid work.

Hipgrave goes on to point out that in some societies there is no concept of adolescence, or that it lasts until an initiation ceremony marking the passage from childhood to adulthood. However, in our society, he states, there is no consistent point at which young people are treated as adults, as the legal age shifts confusingly, varying between activities such as drinking alcohol (18), getting married (18, or 16 with parental consent), remaining in some form of education (18), consenting to sex (16), travelling on public transport, watching films, or committing a crime.

For a young person who has had to "grow up" very quickly in order to fend for themselves or care for their siblings or a vulnerable parent, who has been exposed to sexual activity, violence, drugs and alcohol since early childhood, has had to steal to feed themselves, and has developed a nicotine habit to calm their nerves, many of these legal constraints can seem quite ridiculous. However, that young person may, at the same time, be way behind their peers in terms of emotional intelligence, and be unable to manage their own feelings and the social negotiations their contemporaries have long taken for granted.

In this book, we mainly concentrate on young people between the age of about 11 or 12 (when biological and brain changes tend to start) to around 18 or 19, because that is the age when many young people leave foster care. However, since the introduction of Staying Put legislation in England and Scotland, and the When I'm Ready agreement in Wales[1], there are now more opportunities for young people to continue living with their foster carers after the age of 18, if you both want this.

---

1   Since May 2014, fostered young people in England have the right to stay with their foster families when they reach 18, if both parties agree. Similar schemes exist in Scotland and Wales.

The STAGE Framework

The following framework may be helpful to bear in mind when you are thinking about your approach to fostering teenagers. It is called STAGE because each of the letters represents a key element of the relationship between adults and teenagers.

S is for Significance. Adults can feel that they don't have much influence on teenagers, but research shows that 'without a relationship with a caring and stable adult it is so much harder for a teenager to make a successful transition to adulthood'.

T is for Two-way communication. Good communication involves a two-way process, not just telling or asking. Teenagers really need to feel heard and 'good communication between an adult and a young person involves as much listening as talking'.

A is for Authority. Authority at this stage cannot be the same as during childhood. Authority has to be based on respect and good communication. 'A structure has to be in place but it has to be reasonable and to take into account the age and circumstances of the individual young person.'

G is for Generation gap. This is a reminder that adults can all too easily make judgements that are not based on teenage life today. 'Adults must be careful not to make judgements based on the attitudes of an earlier generation.'

E is for Emotion, which is a reminder that the developing teenage brain needs time to mature and regulate itself. Teenagers have 'the capacity to arouse strong emotions in the adults around them...their feelings may also include elements of sadness, distress and even shame when things go wrong. It is essential for foster carers to receive support in learning to recognise and manage their emotions. It is only in this way that adults can help young people to develop a better means of managing their own feelings.'

Taken from *Teenagers in Foster Care* (Coleman, 2016, p12).

Communication

Good communication is key to everything you do as a foster carer, and again and again, advice in this book will focus on the need to really listen to young people in order to create open discussions – to replace more traditional ways of telling young people what to do. Good listening makes a young person feel that they are being valued as an individual, and that their opinions and feelings are being respected and considered.

As adults, we often think that we are listening but we are also running many other things through our head at the same time, and young people often seem to pick the busiest time to try and start a conversation. If you really don't have time to listen properly to a young person when they want to speak to you, then say so. Explain that, for instance, you have to get them to the bus on time, and that you believe what they have to say is important and you don't want to rush it. You will make time for them later and you will give them your full attention.

When you listen to a young person, be aware that there are several different levels of listening.

- There is a very superficial level, where your thoughts are elsewhere and you're simply "going through the motions".

- There is also a level where you are thinking about how you are going to respond to what is being said.

- And then there is deep listening, which is where you listen to each and every word the young person says to you.

Some people are natural deep listeners, but for many of us it doesn't come easily. Truly listening to someone is one of the best ways to make a person feel respected and valued.

When you listen, you don't need to look straight into the young person's eyes – some will find this very off-putting – but sitting alongside the young person or slightly at an angle, and making sure that your body language is open and inviting, is a good way to encourage them to talk. (Avoid folding your arms or sitting perched on the edge of your chair, as this can seem intimidating or as if you do not have time to fully hear them out.) Some young people can also find it easier to talk if you are doing an activity together, like chopping vegetables or walking side by side, as this takes the direct focus off them. Also, it's good to try and pace the young person in the speed at which you speak. If they are speaking quite fast it can be helpful to respond in a similar way, but then gradually slow the pace down to encourage them to do the same.

A good way to improve your listening skills is to repeat back in your head what is being said to you – it can be surprising what you hear when you do this. You notice the particular words someone else uses, and how often they use them. You need to listen with deep curiosity, wanting to really understand what the young person is saying. Ask open questions, such as 'How do you feel about that?', or 'What would help you?' Try to stick closely to the young person's own words and keep judgement out of your response – if they say 'It was all a bit of a mess', ask 'What would help to sort out the mess?', rather than 'What are you going to do about this awful situation?'

By listening deeply and asking very open questions, you can encourage a young person to start considering new perspectives. For example, when a young person says that they were never wanted by their mother, you could say: 'I can understand why you might feel like this, but I remember you telling me about that time before your mum was ill, when you used to have fun with her... and I wonder if there were times when your relationship was better?' Or when the young person says: 'I've always been rubbish at everything', you could say something like: 'I'm curious about who told you that, because that's not what I see...I see someone very capable and worthwhile and I wonder what stopped other people from seeing that...' However, make sure that you find ways to make these phrases your own, as young people are very good at spotting when you're simply using the latest phrase!

Breaking through young people's armour

Young people in care often develop mental and emotional "armour" to protect and defend themselves, and even in the most caring and supportive environment it is going to take a lot of time and reassurance before they are ready to let go of this protection. You need to ask yourself: what does this young person's self-protective armour look like, and why have they made it like this? Are they shutting down, not needing anyone's help, or are they clinging or demanding your attention all the time? How can you start to find cracks in that armour so that the young person can be unguarded enough to be open to new experiences and opportunities for growth and development? Can you use humour? Can you find ways to make them feel that they're worthy of care and attention?

You probably have your own definition of the "problem/s" you are having with the young person, but what is the young person's definition of the problem? Are you making assumptions about how things are but they're not actually like this at all, from the young person's perspective? Are you trying to achieve things that the young person doesn't understand or doesn't value? Are you undervaluing what really matters to the young person and consequently making them feel that you don't value them? How can you create a shared approach where the young person recognises that you are "on their side", even if you don't always share the same values and aspirations?

> Sensitive caregivers have the capacity to stay in touch with the young person's goals and agenda even if they are very different from those of themselves or other family members. This approach is likely to lead to shared endeavour and an alliance with the young person, rather than a clash of wills and a sense of conflict.

(Schofield and Beek, 2018, p242)

The fostering process

This book is about the issues you may encounter when teenagers are placed with you. Detailed information about the process of preparation to be a foster carer, assessment, and your foster care role and duties can be found in *Thinking About Fostering: The definitive guide to fostering in the UK* (Bond, 2016; published by CoramBAAF). But in brief, in order to foster you need to be accepted by a fostering service that is looking to recruit people with the experiences and attitudes necessary to care for teenagers, and they will then prepare and assess you as a foster carer. Checks and references will also be required. Your application will be put to a fostering panel that will make a recommendation about your suitability as a foster carer to a senior member of the fostering service. If you are approved, you will be given a supervising social worker.

Each young person needing foster care will also have their own social worker – called the child's social worker. Before a young person is placed with you, you will be given an outline of the young person's circumstances and the problems and issues they are likely to face, and you will have a chance to decide if this sounds like a young person you can care for appropriately. If you decide that you feel able to offer this young person a place in your home, you and the young person will be prepared for the young person to move in and you may have a chance to meet them beforehand. However, a lot of placements occur in an emergency and the social worker may not know very much about the young person. In these cases, you will have to apply your skills to find out/meet this young person's needs until more is known. In some cases, you may be offered additional training to help you look after a young person.

You will be expected to sign a foster care agreement for each young person who is placed with you to say that you have understood the work that the service is asking you to do with this young person. You will also be required to keep evidence-based records of the young person's progress, and any meetings and contact that you and the young person have with staff from other services. You should have regular meetings with your supervising social worker and be offered opportunities for professional development and training.

What this book covers

This handbook covers issues such as the development of the teenage brain, managing behaviour, well-being and mental health, issues of identity and how they impact in the adolescent years, and how to support young people in education and through into young adult life.

It won't give you all the answers – many of them you will have to work out for yourself as you identify and respond to the unique needs of the young person who has come to live in your home – but it does bring together a wealth of information, advice and inspiration from a wide range of sources. It will help you to recognise that nobody gets it right all the time, and why even the most experienced foster carers find some placements much harder than others.

You may find yourself rethinking and adapting your parenting style to overcompensate for all the mental injuries this young person is living with. You will need a great deal of patience, a lot of compassion, a lot of self-regulation to manage your own emotions and responses, and a tough skin to ignore the opinions of other people who don't understand why you may let the young person "get away with" behaviours that they wouldn't allow their teenager to get away with (because you're wise enough to know which battles to fight and which to let go).

Nobody claims it's going to be easy, but the outcomes can be hugely rewarding when you begin to see young people making changes to their behaviour, achieving little – or even big – things that matter to them, and starting to live fulfilling young adult lives.

> *Young people can be a delight, they can have new and interesting ideas, challenge your thinking in a good way, be kind and caring sometimes, have good banter, and make great strides in their lives which is very rewarding. They are individual people – not just teenagers.*

(Adam, foster carer)

1 It's all about the brain

During the teenage years, the brain goes through a crucial period of development to prepare us for adulthood. Just before the start of puberty, our brains become highly overproductive, creating many potential new neural pathways. From about the age of 14 until around 25, our brains reinforce the pathways we are likely to need for adulthood and "prune" back the weaker ones. These changes are profound and they also happen to coincide with a time when hormones are causing physical changes in our bodies. It's no wonder that the personalities of teenagers seem to change significantly, and they are full of questions about who they are and what their lives are all about.

In his book, *The Brain: The story of you*, David Eagleman (2015) explains the biological reasons why teenagers tend to be impulsive, more likely to take risks, feel passionately about issues, get easily overwhelmed, and seemingly overreact to situations in ways that adults may find puzzling.

> *Because these massive changes take place in brain areas required for higher reasoning and the control of urges, adolescence is a time of steep cognitive change. The dorsolateral prefrontal cortex, important for controlling impulses, is among the most belated regions to mature, not reaching its adult state until the early twenties.*

(2015, p15)

Some aspects of teenage behaviour may seem especially puzzling and frustrating to adults. A teenager's need to be constantly in touch with their friends, to reach targets on social media or to have the most expensive trainers or designer products may appear excessive and ridiculous. However, the need to be part of a "tribe" is a compelling urge generated by the teenage brain.

In his video, *The Teenage Brain* (www.youtube.com/watch?v=TLULtUPyhog), Daniel Siegel says that it is natural for mammals to seek safety by being with others – this is what allows them to survive. Not being able to have this sense of connection can feel like a matter of "life and death", so when a teenager expresses an urgent need to have a particular kind of shoe or to go to a party with their friends, this is based in an evolutionary drive to belong to the group.

Siegel says that while this doesn't mean we have to give in to everything teenagers ask for, it can help us to have more empathy towards the urgency of their need. They are not simply giving in to peer pressure, but are trying to guarantee their long-term survival.

The additional pressures faced by looked after young people

According to attachment theories – based on the seminal work of John Bowlby and childcare specialists and neuroscientists – a child's resilience (the ability to cope with the changes, stresses and uncertainties of life) is formed by their relationship with their primary carer (usually the mother) during their earliest years. Without a secure attachment during that crucial period, the child lives in a constant state of alarm and arousal. They are unable to tell the difference between real threats and minor stresses, and may be unable to distinguish between excitement and fear.

You may have been fostering a child since their early years and feel that you have done a good job in creating the stability, security and acceptance that this young person needs – but when adolescence occurs, it may feel like all that careful relationship building has vanished. Alternatively, you may be taking in a teenager who has been in a previous stable placement, or who has had multiple placements, or who is in their first placement because family relationships have recently broken down. That young person is bringing all their former history into your home, their confusion and possible distress at being moved and separated from family, friends and former environments, together with the heightened feelings generated by the changes in their brain.

The "pruning" process in the teenage brain can be especially difficult for young people who have experienced trauma in their early lives. The young person may be re-traumatised and previous strategies for managing their feelings may be stripped away.

Childhood defences against too much emotional pain often fail to hold in the teenage years. This is due to all the hormonal, body, brain and psychological changes. This means that early childhood experiences of terror, abandonment, shame or loss, successfully defended against in childhood, can be triggered in intense emotional outbursts and turmoil.

(Siegel, 2014, p90)

Supporting teenagers with attachment difficulties

You will be told about attachment issues in your training as a foster carer, and why poor attachment to a primary carer at an early stage of life can have a serious impact on an individual's development. A young person with attachment difficulties does not trust you to be able to help them, because their previous experiences have taught them that adults cannot be relied on. You are going to have to devote a lot of time and patience to showing them that they are valued, accepted and that their emotional and physical needs can be met.

If you know the young person is only going to be with you for a short time, you may worry about how much you can achieve and whether developing a strong connection might be harmful to the young person, but what you can do is to instil the beginnings of trust in a young person. Your role is not about "fixing" them, but about providing a supportive and stable environment where they can make new discoveries and neural connections and where, gradually, change can happen in the way in which they experience life and the way in which they respond to it.

Your role as a foster carer is to help the young person manage these changes in their brains, while also modelling ways of behaviour that will help them to feel secure, develop trust and recognise that there are different ways of behaving.

Over time, consistent availability, a pervading sense of unconditional positive regard, and a nurturing response to need counter-balance the primary experience of unavailable adults, and promotes the healthy development of self-esteem and self-worth...

...where the inner world of the child is thought about and their primary needs are answered, the planned environment stands symbolically and practically

for the role and function of the attachment figure: to provide the trusting, reliable and sensitive interactions that engender secure attachment.

(Taylor, 2010)

Conditions that affect a young person's processing abilities

There are a range of conditions that are not mental health issues as such, but which may affect a young person's ability to process information, adapt to new situations and fit in with their peers. These conditions can be more common in looked after children than in the general population. They can add additional problems for young people who have experienced trauma, separation and loss and may also affect the way in which they understand and process their history. However, young people with these conditions may also have unique perspectives on life from which others can learn, and can find a lot of pleasure in activities that suit their personality and strengths. Some of these conditions are explored below.

If you are caring for a young person with any condition that affects their ability to process information, you are likely to receive additional information and training about their needs.

Foetal alcohol spectrum disorder (FASD)

In some cases, a child's brain may be affected in the womb by their mother's alcohol use, and this can have a significant effect on their development and functioning. Exposure to alcohol causes damage to the pre-frontal cortex of the foetus's brain. These difficulties may become particularly apparent during the teenage years.

The brain of the alcohol-damaged child is disorganised and the way in which the various parts of the brain connect with and "talk" to each other is slower than in unaffected children. The brain of an affected child needs to work much harder than the brain of an unaffected child in just about everything.

(Mather, 2018)

Symptoms can include hyperactivity, poor judgement, poor planning and organisational skills, failure to consider consequences, short memory span, and impulsivity. Children with this disorder often have very little understanding of risk and can put themselves in situations of serious danger. However, affected children can also be very friendly, loving, loyal, gentle, compassionate and creative.

During the teenage years, carers can play a valuable part in supporting young people with FASD, and can help other people to recognise that the young person is genuinely struggling with everyday issues, rather than being awkward, thoughtless or disobedient. These teenagers can be seen as lazy and unwilling to learn; their impulsiveness, talkativeness and lack of boundaries can make them unpopular with their peers and subject to bullying; and their naivety and inability to assess risks can expose them to being easily led into dangerous situations. Difficulties in school are commonplace.

These young people need a huge amount of routine, consistency and loving support from foster carers who can have positive but realistic expectations for them to realise their potential, and who will open-heartedly celebrate the smallest signs of improvement and development.

Further resources

Mather M (2018) *Dealing with Foetal Alcohol Spectrum Disorders: A guide for social workers*, London: CoramBAAF

Autism Spectrum Disorder (ASD)

> *Autism is a lifelong developmental disability that affects how people perceive the world and interact with others.*

> (National Autistic Society, www.autism.org.uk/about/what-is/asd.aspx#)

Autism can have a range of effects on those who have it. Young people on one "end" of the autism spectrum may be very high functioning and have exceptional talents, whereas at the other "end" they may find it almost impossible to communicate. Common features of ASD include:

- difficulties with social interactions and understanding other people's perspectives;
- a need for routine;

- obsessive, ritualised behaviours and collecting of facts and information;

- reliance on facts, and taking things at a very literal level, e.g. not understanding metaphors such as 'It's raining cats and dogs'.

Young people with autism may also have learning disabilities and/or mental health issues. Some young people with ASD may be very resistant to physical touch and close relationships, but others may be affectionate and very caring.

Further resources

Carter P (2013) *Parenting a Child with Autism Spectrum Disorder*, London: BAAF

The National Autistic Society website has a range of information, including advice for supporting young people during periods of transition. www.autism.org.uk/about/transition.aspx

There are a number of helpful books that explore autism, but novels such as *The Curious Incident of the Dog in the Night Time* (Mark Haddon, Vintage Children's Classics, 2012) and *Marcelo in the Real World* (Francisco X Stork, Scholastic, 2009) can help readers to gain insight into the minds of young people with autism.

Attention Deficit Hyperactivity Disorder (ADHD)

The symptoms of ADHD are usually noticeable before the age of six. Diagnosis has traditionally been more common in boys, perhaps partly due to the fact that boys are more likely to exhibit the hyperactivity that the disorder can involve, and so their condition can be more noticeable. Symptoms can include:

- short attention span and being easily distracted;

- appearing forgetful and losing things;

- not being able to stick to a task;

- appearing to be unable to listen or carry out instructions;

- being unable to sit still or wait for a turn, and constantly fidgeting, talking and interrupting conversations;

- being unable to concentrate and focus, and making careless mistakes;

• acting without thinking and having little or no sense of danger.

Further resources

Jacobs B and Miles L (2012) *Parenting a Child with Attention Deficit Hyperactivity Disorder*, London: BAAF

Understanding their own brains

Teenagers like to feel in control. They also like explanations that are practical and non-patronising.

Blame My Brain: The Amazing Teenage Brain Revealed, by Nicola Morgan, is a highly entertaining, detailed description of how the brain works and how it affects teenage behaviour. It also makes good reading for adults, and can be a great starting point for discussions with fostered teenagers about their behaviour.

Further resources

Forrester D (2012) *Parenting a Child Affected by Parental Substance Misuse*, London: BAAF

Hughes D and Bayon J (2012) *Brain-Based Parenting: The neuroscience of caregiving for healthy attachment*, New York: Norton

Jackson C (2012) *Parenting a Child with Mental Health Issues*, London: BAAF

Morgan N (2013) *Blame My Brain: The amazing teenage brain revealed,* London: Walker

Siegel D (2014) *Brainstorm: The power and purpose of the teenage brain*, London: Scribe

The Teenage Brain, www.youtube.com/watch?v=TLULtUPyhog

2 Identity and belonging

Having a strong sense of who we are and where we belong in the world is fundamental for healthy emotional development. The teenage years are the time when many young people have issues around their sense of identity, as nature prepares them to move away from their dependence on their parents. For young people in foster care, the teenage years can be especially challenging because they already have questions and concerns about who they are and where they belong, accompanied by feelings of rejection and loss.

During your preparation and assessment as a foster carer, you will hear a great deal about the importance of supporting the development of healthy identity in young people who are fostered. You will probably be asked to think about how your own identity formed – how did you develop your sense of belonging, who did you see yourself as, and where did you fit in your family, your school and your community? What was the culture you grew up in, how would you describe your ethnicity, how did your family's religious beliefs, customs and traditions affect your sense of self? You will then be asked to think about how a young person in foster care has developed – or not developed – their sense of self, and how you can support them to feel comfortable and confident about who they are.

This chapter looks at how important it is to help young people in foster care develop as positive and holistic a sense of self as possible. Naturally this is a very complicated subject and further reading is recommended, but here are some of the issues that your fostering service is likely to ask you to focus on.

What is identity?

Sometimes we talk about identity as though it is a fixed thing, but most of us have many facets to our identity. Who we are can change according to whom we are with or the activity we are engaged in. It is common for teenagers to experience confusion around their sense of identity within their own families, peer group and community, but for a young person in care this sense of confusion is likely to be even greater. If the young person is living with a family of a different culture, religion or ethnicity, or if the young person comes from a different country and has no shared knowledge of everyday life in the UK, the confusion may be even more profound.

Identity starts in seeing ourselves reflected in other people, so our families and early experiences create the foundation of our identities. As we grow, we then become more aware of whether we accept or reject aspects of our family identity, especially during the teenage years, when we experience the need to assert our sense of self and are more strongly drawn to identify with our peers. We may challenge religious or cultural beliefs or political views, or just feel irritated by the attitudes and habits of the family members and others around us. But at least we had a sense of being part of that family and knowing what we were reacting against.

Imagine how much more difficult it is for a teenager who is trying to manage the separation from their own family and to adjust to life in your family, and may also have lived in other foster families or residential settings, and is trying to assimilate all of that into their sense of self. Unsurprisingly, many looked after young people have a fractured sense of themselves or feel torn between conflicting loyalties.

Identity works at a deep level, with internal messages that we carry but aren't always aware of. For example, you may have grown up with a parent who said: 'You never give up because you don't know what's round the next corner', which has helped to make you into the resilient person you are today. The young person you foster may have grown up with subtle family messages about: 'Nothing good ever happens to us, so there's no point trying'.

Nurturing a child's heritage

Wherever possible, fostering services try to place young people with foster carers who can meet their needs arising from their ethnicity, culture, religious beliefs and language so that the young person at least has a sense of themselves in a society where others may regard them as a minority, and where they may be subject to racism or bullying about their "differences". It is easier for a young person to feel confident and secure about their identity when messages of reassurance and support can be given by people who share a similar cultural heritage, ethnicity or religious beliefs to the young person. Even if this is the case for you and the young person, you still need to recognise their individuality, and help them to manage issues where their need to assert their independence clashes with cultural or religious values that your family or their family observe. You may need to talk to your supervising social worker about the best ways to manage this.

However, it isn't always possible to find families who share a similar cultural heritage, ethnicity or religion to that of a young person, especially in the case of migrant young people. In these situations, services will look for carers who are adaptable, open-minded and can really understand the young person's sense of confusion, loss and torn loyalties. If you foster young people with a different culture, ethnicity or religion to your own, you need to find out as much as possible about their culture or country of origin, make contact with cultural groups in your local area, and possibly make links with other families fostering young people from that country (but be aware that there can be many factions within a country – you probably don't want to put a young person in contact with people from factions that persecuted their family in their homeland). Use this information to explore the background of the young person's country of origin or cultural practices, but don't assume that the young person will necessarily relate to all of these. Each young person will have their own family traditions and will be developing their own views as an individual.

In all situations, the best approach is to show curiosity about what the young person likes and dislikes, how they see themselves and what is important to them. However, you do need to be aware that migrant young people from other countries may come from environments where secrecy was essential in order to keep themselves and their family safe, so don't be surprised if they are evasive in answering some questions.

Identity around being in care

Young people who have spent some time in foster or residential care may have developed a sense of identity within the care system itself – and feel a natural sense of connection with other looked after young people.

There's a real sense of connection between young people in care – on our weekends away you'd see the most unlikely connections forming…young people who wouldn't talk to each other in normal social situations sitting next to each other on the train and comparing details about their lives, and giving each other a great deal of encouragement and support.

(Ruth, worker with young people)

Having this powerful sense of connection with other looked after young people can be a very positive thing, but it can also lead to conflicts of loyalty, and this is something you need to be aware of.

I met this girl who was fostered, like me, and we just, like, clicked. But her foster carers got to hear I'd got this court case coming up and they didn't want her to have anything to do with me. They really got heavy about it and she ran away from home one time...Then the whole thing fell apart and she got moved to another family. We kind of lost touch but I heard that she'd got a baby with this guy who was forcing her to go with older men and stuff. Last year I heard that she took an overdose and she didn't pull through...I feel so crap...like I let her down...I've not been sleeping and I've started drinking again.

(Nathan, 21)

It's also important to recognise that some young people may react strongly to being labelled as being "in care" and may not want to be associated with other looked after children and young people.

Our young person was horrified by being defined as a "looked after child" and never wanted to attend any of the days out or holiday get-togethers organised by his agency. We were given permission by his agency allowing him not to sign for his pocket money, which was a massive thing for him.

(Foster carer)

Sexuality and sexual identity

During the teenage years, nature can give young people strong messages about getting ready to be reproducers of future generations, and they are ready to explore their identity as sexual beings. It is no wonder that young people often struggle with the boundaries around sexual activity placed on them by the legal system and by adults around them. For young people in foster care, there may be additionally confusing issues about sexual activity that they witnessed in their birth families, or sexual abuse or exploitation they have experienced themselves.

Reproduction is only one element of sexuality, and sexual orientation and who you are attracted to, who you love and who you identify with in society are all important aspects of a young person's sexual identity. You may be familiar with the term LGBT – referring to Lesbian, Gay, Bisexual and Transgender, but terminology changes all the time as people look for ways to be recognised for who they are. Increasingly, terms like LGBTI are being used – where the I is used to refer to Intersex for people whose bodies don't conform to standard male/female anatomy. You may also come across the term LGBTIQA – where the Q is used to identify people who have reclaimed the word "Queer" to refer to being "Gender Queer", meaning that they don't identify as male or female, or consider themselves to be a combination of genders, or feel themselves to be between or beyond gender definitions. The A stands for "Asexual", which includes people with low sexual interest as well as those with no sexual interest. You may find these new definitions of identity challenging (especially if you have spent a long time struggling to have your own sexual identity accepted within society), but you need to recognise that the young person's need to identify and feel a sense of belonging takes priority over your personal opinions.

(For information about promoting sexual health, see Chapter 4.)

Further resources

The **Albert Kennedy Trust** was set up to support young people who are LGBT and homeless. It provides a range of support, and youth engagement programmes for LGBT young people.
www.akt.org.uk/

Stonewall provides information and support about LGBT+ issues, including ways to support young people. Stonewall Youth also provides information about local activities and sources of support for young people.
www.youngstonewall.org.uk/

Befrienders is an international organisation that provides emotional support to prevent suicide worldwide. It also has a range of resources about sexual orientation.
www.befrienders.org/about-sexual-orientation

Disability

Many young people in foster care will have disabilities – whether these are conditions they are born with, such as Foetal Alcohol Syndrome, Autism, Down's Syndrome, physical disabilities from birth or caused by accidental or non-accidental injury. Although mental health issues are not always classified under disability, some young people may have developed a severe mental health problem (probably related to trauma) during their childhood that has a lasting impact on their ability to function in society.

For many young people, realising that they are not the only ones experiencing this condition or mental or physical injury can be a huge relief. Being with, or having communication or connections with, others who experience the same issues as they do can provide support and create a sense of solidarity – which may have a positive impact on a young person's sense of identity, and can help them cope better with difficult situations.

> *Disability identity refers to possessing a positive sense of self and feelings of connection to, or solidarity with, the disability community. A coherent disability identity is believed to help individuals adapt to disability, including navigating related social stresses and daily hassles.*
>
> *Identities help people make sense of different and distinct parts of their self-concepts. For people with disabilities, an identity should contain relevant content and goals linked to disability. In effect, disability identity should guide people with disabilities towards what to do, what to value and how to behave in those situations where their disability stands out, as well as those where it is not salient.*
>
> (Dunn D and Burcaw S (2013) 'Thinking about disability identity: major themes of disability identity are explored', *Spotlight on Disability* newsletter, American Psychological Association, www.apa.org/pi/disability/resources/publications/newsletter/2013/11/disability-identity)

Some areas of the disability world have very clearly defined cultures. For example, Deaf culture has its own social beliefs, history, values, art and literary traditions, and it can be very helpful for young people who are deaf to be placed with carers who are part of this culture. Not all disabilities have such a strong sense of culture and obviously not all young people can be linked to carers who have the same disability, but it's important for them to be placed with people who believe in their potential, and who are prepared to help them to feel accepted and valued in their identity as a disabled person.

If you have a disability yourself, have experienced mental health issues or have overcome serious difficulties in your life, you can play an important role in helping young people to understand the benefits of persistence, resilience and determination; and recognise the advantages and strengths of being different from mainstream society.

Further resources

Disability Matters for Foster Carers provides a wealth of information about disabled children and young people's health and the lived experience of disability.
www.disabilitymatters.org.uk/Component/Details/468756

Carter P (2013) *Parenting a Child with Autism*, London: BAAF

Forrester D (2012) *Parenting a Child Affected by Parental Substance Misuse*, London: BAAF

Jackson C (2012) *Parenting a Child with Mental Health Issues*, London: BAAF

Family identity

Young people's loyalties can be strongly divided between members of their birth family and foster family. They may be very protective of their birth family and feel a need to strongly align themselves with them and their values and behaviours. Or they may, being teenagers, feel a real sense of disconnection from their birth family and want to be seen as part of your family instead. Some birth families will work very positively with foster carers, recognising that you are providing the support that they can't manage during a time of illness or family breakdown. Conversely, in some situations birth family members may be resentful of the foster family and may try to sabotage the relationship you are trying to build with the young person. Relatives might bring expensive presents to contact visits to prove that they can provide for the young person better than you can, or a birth family member might encourage the young person to steal from your family or reject your family, in order to prove their loyalty. This can seriously upset a young person who is trying to manage their dual role as a member of both families.

You can help the young person by letting them know that you recognise it can be difficult in their situation (but don't say 'I know how you feel' – nobody likes being told how they feel and teenagers can be extremely sensitive to this). Encourage them to think about all the skills and abilities they have and to remember times when they have had to adapt to difficult situations, and how they can use similar skills to manage conflicts they currently feel. How can they reinforce their sense of loyalty to their birth family, but without behaving in ways which disrupt their placement with your foster family? Can they recognise that in being adaptable and resilient, they are developing skills that create a strong sense of themselves?

Contact issues

It is difficult to separate issues of identity and permanence. It is the fact of having two families, one born into and another one that the child is a full member of, that makes adopted and permanently fostered children feel different from other children. Making sense of two life narratives will impact on children and adopted adults in different ways but the identity of having two families cannot be separated from questions about contact.

(Adams, 2012, p7)

Contact has an important role in helping young people to maintain relationships with key people and develop a healthy sense of their identity. Remember that "contact" has a number of aspects – it isn't just about meeting or speaking with parents, siblings or other relatives, or "keeping the doors open" for the future, but is also about keeping memories and histories alive to give the young person a sense of their "building blocks", who they were and who they are now, and where many of their belief systems and values come from. It is about creating an environment in which the young person can talk openly about their family, and is able to express both the positives and negatives they feel, and is able to raise any questions they have. It is also about creating a space in which they can "keep people in mind", even when they cannot have contact with them.

A young person may have existing contact arrangements that have worked well during their childhood, but in the teenage years their feelings towards contact may change significantly. They may strongly reject the idea of other people having a say in who they see and how, when and where they see them.

They may be keen to keep contact with their siblings but unwilling to have contact with their parents at this time, as they may feel a sense of rejection or abandonment more painfully during these years and have angry feelings towards them. Conversely, contact may become very important to them because they have a strong need to ask questions about their identity, culture and history.

If the young person is likely to be returning home, then maintaining contact will be important, and you may need to be creative and supportive in enabling this to happen. For a long-term placement, it may be appropriate to respect the young person's wishes and allow them to have a break from contact if they really don't want it at this point.

> Our social worker gave us wise advice about contact – to keep things on a professional basis when dealing with birth families. Remembering that we have a job to do for the child and that's our priority, rather than feeling we have to become their friends.

(Phil, foster carer of teenagers)

Remember that in this age of social media, contact can take place in a number of ways. In *Foster Care and Social Networking: A guide for social workers and foster carers*, Eileen Fursland points out:

> Where contact has been agreed and is in the child's best interests, new communications technologies can provide tremendous benefits by making it easier and cheaper to keep in touch – and these are the ways in which children and young people often feel most comfortable communicating. Contact does not just mean face-to-face meetings and phone calls: it can also include emails, texts, instant-messaging, Skype and social networking.

(Fursland, 2011, p49)

Supporting the young person with their identity

In all these situations, the key to helping a young person develop a healthy sense of identity is open communication. Rather than making assumptions about what is going on for them, you need to create situations where you can help the young person to identify and communicate their own experiences and feelings and develop your own understanding of what it's like for them.

With younger children or children with learning disabilities, life story work can be a good way to open up conversations about how they see themselves and their history. Life story work can also be undertaken very sucessfully with older children and young people – see *Digital Life Story Work* (Hammond and Cooper, 2013) for a range of imaginative ideas and projects. As a foster carer of teenagers, you may feel that you don't have permission to talk to young people about these issues, that it's the social worker's job, but it can be empowering for young people to realise that their foster carer is interested in their opinions and experiences.

Further resources

Bond H (2007) *Ten Top Tips for Managing Contact*, London: BAAF

3 Keeping young people safe

Fostering extends beyond the parameters of your own home, and beyond the duties to provide shelter, food and clothing for a young person. One of your key roles as a carer is to anticipate and look out for circumstances and situations where a young person could be at risk.

Taking risks is a natural behaviour for many teenagers and, for young people in care, pushing the boundaries through risk-taking is often one of the ways in which they may explore their identity, bond with peers, but also express the hurt inside themselves that has resulted from their difficult earlier experiences.

Managing risk for a young person can be stressful for you, and it is important to make sure that you have enough support for yourself. Is there another professional or carer with whom you can share your worries and who can offer advice? You also need to recognise that a young person's risk-taking behaviour is unlikely to be a reflection of your ability to look after them, so don't be hard on yourself if things go wrong. (Read more about looking after yourself in Chapter 6.)

> *It's hard to give foster carers the message that they need to accept a level of normality in these behaviours for a young person who is exploring their identity, their pain and their belonging, whilst at the same time not being dismissive of the risks of teenage behaviour and the need to keep talking/ thinking about what is going on, and how to keep communicating with the teen.*

(Manager of an independent fostering agency)

Risk assessment and risk management

When a young person moves into your home, a risk assessment will be conducted to consider the best way of keeping that young person safe. It must be specific to the individual young person and your personal circumstances and environment. This should be done by your supervising social worker and the child's social worker, in consultation with you and the young person, prior to the young person being placed. You should be given all the information you need in order to keep this young person safe in your care. In the case of an emergency placement, the young person may not be involved in the assessment and it may be undertaken by phone or email, because of the urgency of the situation.

All arrangements, including risk assessments, should be reviewed at regular periods, such as 72 hours after an emergency placement or the one-month looked after review.

Areas of risk that will be reviewed include:

- risks from other children/young people already in placement;
- risks to other children or young people in the household (this could include grandchildren or neighbours' children);
- risks arising from the young person's disability or health issues, such as medication;
- risks from the young person's self-harm and drug and alcohol misuse;
- risks from the young person's sexual behaviour;
- risks from the young person running away, or getting involved in gangs or child sexual exploitation (CSE);
- risks from the young person's family members;
- risks from the young person being abducted;
- risks associated with the young person fire setting.

Risks are usually rated as low, medium or high and can affect whether or not a young person is placed with you (or remains with you in the case of an emergency placement). You should be given training, support, advice and specialist equipment where this is needed to help you manage these risks. If you are concerned that you cannot keep a young person safe, or need extra support to do this, you should contact your supervising social worker.

Safer caring

As part of your preparation for fostering, you will learn about providing safer care. This describes ways of looking after the young person that will keep them safe, and will protect them from situations that might remind them of times when they were abused or which they might misinterpret as being abusive. It's also about keeping yourself safe – to prevent a young person making allegations against you and your family, by avoiding situations that might be mistaken as abusive.

To keep yourself and other members of your household as safe as possible from allegations of abuse, make sure that you keep factual, up-to-date records of the young person's behaviour and your interactions with them.

Sexually abused children

Sexual abuse may have occurred in the young person's birth family, but their vulnerability may have also made them targets for adults outside the home or for other young people in residential care or foster homes. Social workers will not always know whether a young person has experienced this type of abuse.

The teenage years and changes in the brain may cause a young person to revisit the traumas that they experienced at a much younger age, and from which you may feel you have already helped them to move on. A young person coming to live with you may display extremely sexualised behaviour, which may involve targeting your or your partner or other children in the home. Young people may want to disclose abuse to you, or they may struggle with their emerging sexuality. Some young people may have learned to dissociate to manage the trauma of their experiences.

This is a complex and sensitive issue that cannot be covered in depth here, but generally the young person will need very supportive and caring responses to help them manage feelings of shame, and to develop a sense of positive self-esteem. And, as ever, their feelings are likely to be shown in their behaviour. Be aware that caring for a sexually abused child may awaken difficult memories for you, and be prepared to seek help for yourself if you are struggling to manage them.

Further resources

Slade J (2012) *Safer Caring: A new approach*, London: Fostering Network

Youell B (2016) *Parenting a Child Affected by Sexual Abuse*, London: CoramBAAF

PACE UK provides support and a variety of resources to parents and carers of sexually exploited children.
https://paceuk.info/

Child sexual exploitation

In her book, *Caring for a Child who has been Sexually Exploited*, Eileen Fursland explains:

> *Child sexual exploitation can take many forms. Girls are groomed to believe that they are in a loving relationship – until the "boyfriend" starts to demand she has sex with his friends and associates. Boys are being trapped in situations where they are forced to have sex with many men, and threatened and attacked if they try to get out. Both girls and boys are sexually abused by other young people in street gangs. In many cases, child sexual exploitation (CSE) involved serious violence and in some cases, it also involved trafficking of several children or young people by organised groups of older men.*

> (2017, p1)

Young people who have experienced sexual exploitation may not fit the "usual profile" of looked after children, and while parental relationships may be severely damaged (parents may have rejected the young person because of what they've been involved in), they are less likely to be in care because of parental neglect or abuse. If you are going to foster a young person who has been previously sexually exploited then you should be given specialist training for this, but unfortunately this may not be provided in your area. The guide mentioned above can provide some information.

You also need to know how to recognise sexual exploitation and protect young people from it while they are living with you.

Young people who have been sexually abused in the past, who have low self-esteem and crave affection, who don't communicate well, or who are vulnerable because of their disabilities, can be particularly vulnerable to sexual exploitation. Social isolation and recent bereavement or loss can also make young people vulnerable, as can feeling rejected or confused by their sexual identity. This vulnerability should be highlighted in the risk assessment, but you shouldn't hesitate to contact your social worker if you have any concerns. It can be hard to distinguish some of the signs of CSE from normal teenage activity, but some of the things to look out for are:

- going missing from home;

- repeated sexually transmitted infections and/or pregnancies;

- physical injuries;

- poor mental health;

- self-harm or thoughts of suicide;

- receiving presents from unknown sources;

- having a boyfriend/girlfriend who is considerably older than them, or being picked up in a car by an older man.

What these young people need is carers who are listening and non-judgemental, who are prepared to spend a lot of time helping the young person to experience supportive and trusting relationships after the abuse of trust they've experienced through sexual exploitation. As their carer, you must be able to accept and support the young person whether or not they recognise the harmful situation they are in. Some young people may believe they are responsible for their abuse, because they don't understand the "predatory" behaviour of abusers.

A "strengths-based approach", that focuses on the young person's strengths and resources, and seeks to build their interests, motivations and abilities, can provide some help to aid the young person to move on from their abuse.

Further resources

Fursland E (2017) *Caring for a Child who has been Sexually Exploited*, London: CoramBAAF

Fursland E (2009) *Caring for a Young Person who has been Trafficked*, London: BAAF

Youell B (2016) *Parenting a Child Affected by Sexual Abuse*, London: CoramBAAF

The **NSPCC** provides some useful basic information on child sexual exploitation.
www.nspcc.org.uk/preventing-abuse/child-abuse-and-neglect/child-sexual-exploitation/

Gangs

For fostered young people struggling with many aspects of their identity and attachment needs, gangs can offer a very appealing way to create a sense of belonging. Gang life may also have been something their family or friends have been involved with. Being a gang member may give them a sense of feeling powerful, or offer them protection against bullying. Unfortunately, most gang involvement comes with major downsides of violence, drug dealing, sexual violence, knife crime, and the use of other illegal weapons.

Karl Heinz Brisch, writing in *Teenagers and Attachment: Helping adolescents engage with life and learning*, suggests that there may be a link between some forms of poor attachment, behaviour disorders and becoming involved with gangs. He suggests that young people with attachment disorders don't tend to know how to express their concerns or how to ask for help – so instead they may pick verbal and physical fights. Because of their own fears, they use the gang to back them up, rather than attacking someone on their own.

> When several adolescents with this pattern of attachment disorder with aggressive behaviour band together, they frequently form gangs that serve the purpose of protection so that each individual gang member experiences less anxiety – all of which is turned outward. Group loyalty is enforced absolutely, and this is the price paid for group protection. The result is pathological attachment to the other group members.
>
> (Brisch, 2009, p23)

It is no wonder, then, that gangs look to pick fights with others who are not in their gang, or who, worse still, can be seen to belong to another gang, and whose loyalties lie elsewhere. This can be as simple as a geographical division, and you may hear young people from neighbouring towns, counties or postcode areas describing a very active hatred towards anyone who lives on the other side of the border they have created and are desperate to reinforce.

If you notice that the young person you are fostering seems to have a lot of money or items like very expensive trainers, and seems to be using drugs, these could be signs that they are involved with a gang. Again, this is an issue that you have to address by thinking about what part of their needs a gang addresses. What else might meet that need? How can you open up a conversation to discuss this with them? What help and support can you get to do this? Is there support through their school or local projects? Can your supervising social worker suggest training or local support schemes? You need to recognise that gang membership can provide many positives for young people and it can take time, patience and a lot of discussion for them to recognise the serious downsides of this form of belonging.

As a foster carer, you have a duty to the well-being of the young person but you also have a duty to keep other children and young people safe. If you suspect that a young person is putting someone else in danger or is keeping weapons in your house, then you should take action, such as contacting your supervising social worker, or the police.

Further resources

The **NSPCC** has a dedicated section on their website and a video about gangs. www.nspcc.org.uk/preventing-abuse/keeping-children-safe/staying-safe-away-from-home/gangs-young-people/

It also offers advice and support through its helpline: 0808 800 5000

Catch 22, a children's social care charity, also has information about gangs. www.catch-22.org.uk/offers/gangs/#approach

Radicalisation

We see horror stories on the news about radicalised young people committing atrocities, and this has led to some carers being reluctant to care for migrant young people, especially boys. This is an issue that needs to be kept in perspective.

Young people may become radicalised for many reasons, including because they feel isolated, worry about their sense of identity, or are uncomfortable with clashes in values between their cultural or religious beliefs and those of others. Young people becoming significantly more interested in cultural or religious practices, or in politics may be an indicator, but may also be a natural part of their personal development and need to express their identity. It isn't just young people whose families originally came from outside the UK who may be radicalised – white British young people may be influenced by extremist views, finding a new identity for themselves in other cultures and religions, or by joining far-right political groups. Research suggests that far-right extremism is now a significant reason why people are referred to Prevent.[1]

Signs that a young person is at risk of being radicalised include becoming isolated from their peers; having strong, dogmatic views; using aggressive extremist language; showing an increase in intensity of their religious or cultural practices; and spending excessive amounts of time online (none of these are conclusive but taken together may be an indication). However, many young people have strong views at this age so it is not unusual for them to feel disenchanted with society, and there can be real positives in the energy behind this. Young people will often share their views with someone whom they respect, such as a foster carer or teacher.

Here are some suggestions for how to help a young person you are worried about:

- Listen to young people and try to see the world from their perspective.

- Help them understand how to question and debate issues.

- Use online resources – the Prevent package at www.elearning.prevent. homeoffice.gov.uk/edu/screen2.html is accessible and culturally sensitive.

- Be supportive of their desire for justice and help them to find alternative ways to express this.

- Your local authority can offer access to a collaborative package of support (from organisations like the Channel[2] safeguarding board which can help to

---

1   Prevent is the support organisation which is part of the UK's Counter Terrorism Strategy, which works to stop individuals from getting involved with or supporting terrorism or extremist activity.

2   Channel is a programme which focuses on providing support at an early stage to people who are identified as being vulnerable to being drawn into terrorism.

assess and recommend care packages. Channel referral doesn't show up in a young person's records).

- Encourage young people to join local organisations supporting young people from their cultural background.

Further resources

Childline has a helpful section on its website for young people who are concerned about world issues and issues around radicalisation. https://bit.ly/2CR3cHw

Social media

Social media is a central part of young people's lives and very much part of their identity in the 21st century. It is the main way in which many young people communicate, through sites such as Instagram, Snapchat, Facebook, and messaging services. However, it can also be a means whereby young people can be exposed to risks, including being groomed online. To deny access to social media is to cut off young people from friendships and expose them to ridicule for being outside the "norm". At a time when their brains are giving them powerful messages about the need to be part of peer groups (evolution's way of guiding them towards survival in the adult world), denying them access to social media can be deeply distressing for young people. It's important, therefore, to develop your own understanding of how it works and to recognise its benefits, as well as learning how to protect young people from its risks.

Benefits versus risks

If you aren't much of a fan of social media, it may be helpful to know some of the benefits for young people:

- being the same as their peers, i.e. not singled out as different;
- maintaining friendships with former schoolfriends, young people they've met in previous placements or through activities;
- being able to use social media for contact arrangements (see previous section);

- being able to access lots of helpful online advice on issues around safe sex, drugs, self-harm, depression, etc; young people who won't ask for help can access this for themselves;

- being able to correspond with some support organisations through messages or secure Facebook groups;

- accessing valuable peer support from others in similar situations.

A young care leaver posts something on Facebook about feeling depressed or lonely and there's a volley of messages – from others in similar situations but also from workers like me, they've come across over the years. There'll be lots of responses saying 'Let's meet up' or 'I'll give you a call'. It can be incredibly supportive.

(Social care professional)

The downsides of social media can't be overlooked, and you need to be aware of these and make sure that teenagers are aware of the associated risks:

- cyberbullying – this can be very vicious and has led to some suicides;

- sexual exploitation – contact through social media is often a contributory factor in grooming for sexual exploitation;

- radicalisation or exposure to extremist ideologies and viewpoints;

- "sexting" and sharing of sexually explicit photos – these may then be used to bully or blackmail;

- access to gambling sites;

- downloading inappropriate games for their age;

- contact from or with birth family members that may be unwanted or harmful;

- gangs recruit online and may use social media to sell drugs and incite fights.

It is easier to monitor the social media use of younger children, but as young people reach the teenage years, they are likely to know more about this than you do. Also, you cannot monitor what they see on friend's phones or tablets, and it's hard to prevent them receiving calls. Some carers of younger teenagers use methods such as requiring their young people to hand in their phones at a certain time of night so they can check them, but this may not be something you feel comfortable doing, especially if this is an older young person who may deeply resent this intrusion into their privacy. However, you could consider making this a family-wide activity, as there is increasing awareness that use of tablets and mobile phones in the hours before sleep may not be conducive to a good night's rest. It will also seem less punitive if adults are doing it too!

The best way to respond to these issues is to create an environment where young people feel able to talk to you about their lives. Try to familiarise yourself as much as possible with social media used by young people, so they don't get frustrated trying to explain the basics to you when they really want to tell you how a post, message, photo or text has made them feel. You could get your young person to show you themselves, and use this as an opportunity to start a discussion. Better than lecturing them about what not to do, ask them about what they already know and what they think the risks are; what they would do in certain situations; or how they would protect a younger child from the dangers of the internet (this can help you to explain why, as their foster carer, you have concerns about their safety). Try and talk to them as and when issues come up, for example, in the news or in a TV soap opera. Also, make it very clear that, whatever situation they find themselves in, you will not judge them, but will support them to resolve the situation.

Further resources

Fursland E (2011) *Foster Care and Social Networking: A guide for social workers and foster carers*, London: BAAF

Fursland E (2013) *Social Networking and You: A guide for young people*, London: BAAF

Degamo J (2014) *Keeping Foster Children Safe Online: Positive strategies to prevent cyberbullying, inappropriate contact, and other digital dangers*, London: Jessica Kingsley Publishers

The **NSPCC** and the phone company O^2 have created a range of online resources for parents and carers – www.net-aware.org.uk/. This includes information about their downloadable app, NetAware, which is a simple guide for parents to the most popular social networks, apps and games. It also explains the privacy settings and safety guidelines for Facebook, Instagram, Snapchat and others. A free helpline also provides advice about social networking: 0808 8005002.

4 Promoting health and well-being

As a foster carer, you will be expected to help young people develop good practices around keeping themselves as healthy as possible. This can include encouraging them to take part in exercise, find new hobbies, make friends, create a positive relationship with food, develop healthy attitudes and safe practices around sex and sexuality, and around drugs, alcohol and smoking.

Resilience theory

Promoting health and well-being can have a positive effect on young people's resilience. Resilience theory – which is the result of more than 40 years of research into this area – can help us to understand why some young people cope better with difficulties than others. This can be due to the nature of the difficulties, the qualities and experiences of the young person, and the qualities of the relationships and environment in which the young person is growing up. There is also evidence to suggest that having "protective factors" in life (such as hobbies, friendships, sports activities, days out and holidays) can help young people to cope more effectively with difficult and painful experiences. Young people also need opportunities to have positive experiences in their lives, to reinforce their sense of self-esteem – as someone who is "worthy" of these good experiences.

Friendship network

As described earlier in this guide, teenagers have an evolutionary need to be with their peers. However, some young people will find friendships difficult because they have conditions – such as foetal alcohol spectrum disorder or autism – that may make it difficult for them to understand the nuances of social interactions, and they may be shunned or ridiculed by their peers. Also, some young people in care have grown up distrusting others, or have never learned how to develop relationships. They may have friends who are involved in criminal activities, and part of your role as a foster carer is to protect them from negative influences and help them make more healthy connections.

The best way to find out who a young person is mixing with is to ask them to bring their friends home. In that way, you get to meet them and develop a sense of whether they are likely to be a positive or negative influence.

There may be many reasons why a young person doesn't have a network of friends, and simply taking them along to social situations is unlikely to work. Spending time helping young people to develop their communication skills, learn to express their feelings, manage their anger, and develop empathy and social skills based around compromise and tact can be very important. Finding activities where a young person can meet others who share similar interests, or groups where there are other young people with similar disabilities, can often help a "loner" to start making friends. Physical challenges can be a great way of bringing young people together. Meeting up with other young people in care can also be beneficial as they recognise similarities in experience. But remember: friendship is a two-way process, and however much you support a young person, it is ultimately outside your control as to whether other young people respond to their overtures of friendship.

Online friendships are very much a part of current teenage life, and for some young people, having "Facebook friends" may give them a sense of belonging, even if they aren't friends as you might consider them. As with other "friendships", find ways to ask the young person about who they are talking to online and what sort of interests they have in common with these people.

Exercise and leisure activities

Several studies from the UK and abroad have suggested that engagement in sporting activities can open new social relationships beyond the care system...Hollingworth (2012) found that sport for those living in, or leaving care, enabled them to develop friendships and widen their social network, as well as mix and socialise in mainstream activities with young people who are not in care. This is particularly important for looked after children who, due to past experiences, may find interacting with wider networks and communities particularly difficult.

(Quarmby, 2014)

Getting a teenager away from their phone or online games to take exercise can be a real challenge, and the activities we see as pleasurable – such as a walk in the countryside – may seem extremely dull to a young person. While it is important to set a good example to a teenager (they're unlikely to be inspired by you if you constantly fail to use your gym membership or go everywhere by car), you also need to recognise that they may not know about the wide range of activities open to them. You need to become aware of what's on offer in your area, and look for more unusual activities that the young person can do by themselves, with friends, or with your own children. But don't just assume that they will want to do what your family does – your family may love swimming but this young person may have hated it at school and be much more excited by skateboarding, archery or salsa dancing.

Research suggests that young people have often given up a sport because of a move into or through foster care, so ask what they have enjoyed in the past and might like to do again. They may not have considered that it is possible to restart an activity or join a new group.

Of course, activities don't have to be sport-related to be helpful in promoting a young person's well-being. Drama groups, choirs, learning to produce and edit music, photography groups and internet groups at the local library are just a few of hundreds of activities you can find when you start researching.

Also, find out what is specifically available for looked after young people – there may be free leisure centre passes or significant discounts available, and the young person's "leisure allowance" provided by the local authority can be used to help them access activities.

Healthy eating

There's a lot of information available online, and leaflets available from GPs' surgeries, about healthy eating, and it's not unusual to find opinions that contradict. You will probably have your own ideas about what constitutes a healthy diet for a young person, and this often won't match with what the young person chooses to eat themselves. At the same time, you need to be aware that young people – predominantly girls, but increasingly boys too – can be prone to eating disorders, and although they are unfortunately more likely to respond to peer pressure or media images of the "perfect body" than anything you say, you don't want to contribute to these problems by pressurising them to watch their weight or to put on weight. It's much better to create an environment in which conversations about food and healthy nutrition can take place – and there are often documentaries on TV or information online that you can make use of. If the young person sees that you and other family members have healthy, open-minded attitudes to trying new foods and sensibly limiting intakes of sugar, salt and fats, they are more likely to benefit from this than from being banned from eating certain foods or "lectured" about what is good for them.

> *Our foster daughter was a chicken nugget and chips girl when she first came to us but we started watching some documentaries about where food comes from, and she was totally horrified. Now she's as passionate as anyone else about making sure we get free-range eggs and line-caught tuna, and avoid additives and colourings.*
>
> (Foster carer)

Your aim should be to make sure that the young person has a comfortable relationship with food, knows about different food types and what constitutes a balanced and healthy diet – and can weigh up information and make their own choices. It is also important to ensure that they can express their feelings and have people to talk to, rather than "eating down their feelings", or comfort eating. Young people from chaotic family backgrounds may not be used to family mealtimes and some young people may feel very uncomfortable eating in front of others. This might also be the sign of an eating disorder.

The most common forms of eating disorder are anorexia nervosa, bulimia, binge eating disorder and OFSED (other specified feeding or eating disorder). The last category is the most common. Symptoms range from having very rigid routines around food, spending time worrying about weight and body shape, avoiding eating with other people, exercising excessively, eating very little or eating far too much, mood swings, digestive problems, feeling tired, cold or dizzy, and young women may stop having periods. GPs are usually the first point of referral for someone with an eating disorder, but you will need to involve the young person's social worker, especially if they are reluctant to seek help.

Be aware that some young people may have food intolerances (usually limited to digestive problems, although they can be more serious) or allergies (immune system reactions that affect numerous organs in the body, and can be fatal). Information about this should be made available to you by the young person's social worker, and it is good practice to find out as much as you can.

If you suspect that a young person has an undiagnosed allergy, there is helpful information online provided by organisations such as the Food Standards Agency (http://allergytraining.food.gov.uk/english/food-allergy-facts.aspx).

You also need to be aware that food can be a sensitive issue and you should avoid making comments that might be seen as judgemental of young people's birth families or former foster carers. There are also cultural issues – especially if you are fostering young people from other countries or cultures. A young person might be delighted for you to cook them a traditional meat dish from their country of origin, but that young person might also be a vegetarian or have religious beliefs that prohibit certain types of meat. It is better to talk with the young person about what they like to eat and maybe look at some recipes together, or take them shopping with you to observe their reactions to different foods.

Further resources

The **NHS website** has useful advice about the nutritional needs of teenagers. www.nhs.uk/live-well/eat-well/healthy-eating-for-teens/

Beat, an eating disorder charity, has a great deal of information on its website, and a helpline, youthline and student line.
www.beateatingdisorders.org.uk/

Drugs and alcohol

Most teenagers will experiment with drugs and alcohol at some point, however much you try to protect them. Be clear with the young person about why you are imposing certain rules and tell them about legal implications, but try to create an environment where the young person can talk to you even if they have broken these rules, for example, feeling able to call you if they have got drunk or feel scared or unwell after taking drugs.

Alcohol

The average age for teenagers in the UK to try alcohol is 13, and it's often considered a normal part of teenage exploration. However, there is evidence that alcohol can damage developing brains and it can also leave teenagers vulnerable to unsafe situations – such as sexual assault, road and drowning accidents – and can make them more likely to commit criminal behaviour. There is also greater risk of alcohol poisoning at a young age. General medical advice is that if children are given alcohol, then it should definitely not be under the age of 15.

There are also legal issues which you and young people in your care need to be aware of. It is against the law for someone to sell alcohol to anyone under 18, or for anyone below that age to buy or attempt to buy alcohol. However, in licensed premises where someone aged 16 or 17 is accompanied by an adult, they may be allowed to drink, but not buy, beer, wine or cider with a table meal (but this can depend on the licensing arrangement for the premises or the activities taking place there). It is not illegal for a child aged over five to drink alcohol on private premises.

If a young person is caught, by the police, with alcohol three times, they could face a social contract, a fine or arrest, and could end up with a criminal record that could affect their future job prospects and make it more difficult for them to travel to certain countries, such as the US.

You may have personal views about alcohol and may believe it is better to introduce young people to alcohol at home, for example, giving a young person a small glass of wine on a special occasion. It is a good idea to discuss this with your supervising social worker, as this may be strictly against agency policy, but also might lead to accusations from a birth parent that you are encouraging their child to get drunk. You also need to be sensitive to the fact that alcohol is not acceptable in some cultures and religions.

Further resources

Drinkaware has advice on talking to young people about alcohol use, such as how to react to underage drinking at parties.
www.drinkaware.co.uk/advice/underage-drinking/

Forrester D (2012) *Parenting a Child Affected by Parental Substance Misuse*, London: BAAF

Drugs

Be informed about drugs yourself, so you know what young people are likely to take, and how harmful various drugs may be. Young people aren't likely to listen to you if you're uninformed and out of touch with current reality. Some sources of information are listed below.

Young people may take drugs because of natural curiosity, peer pressure or because they are looking for ways to manage their emotions or cope with painful memories from the past. They may not be aware that most drugs come with risks to mental health, which could make their situation worse.

There is a lot of advice about what to do if you suspect a young person is using drugs. The most consistent advice is to avoid hunting through a young person's possessions because this can seriously damage trust, and instead to find ways to open up a conversation with the young person about drugs. If you do find anything that looks like drugs in a young person's clothes or their room, it is recommended that you ask the young person directly about this, rather than contacting the police. A young person may be defiant or strongly deny that this is anything to do with them, and don't be surprised if they refuse to tell you anything about what you have found. Your best course may be to flush the product down the toilet after you have asked the young person about it, because you could be subject to prosecution if it was found. However, it is best to be clear about the policies and procedures of your fostering service and to ask for advice from your supervising social worker if you have concerns.

> *You have to model behaviour around drugs and alcohol. I have bottles of alcohol which have been in my pantry for a long time. We might have two glasses of wine on a Friday night or for a special occasion...I also talk to young people about how drugs and alcohol affect the lives of people they know...If they do drink and get sick then I don't get angry but talk to them about what drove them to that behaviour. Don't be afraid of drugs, be educated about them. Don't tell kids horror stories because they will probably have seen their friends using them. Drugs are easily available and it's likely that young people will try them at some point or other. If they're trying to deny it I say, 'I know you've been trying drugs because your pupils are telling me...so let's sit down and talk about this.*

(Anya, experienced foster carer)

Further resources

Frank, a drug advice charity, has an informative, accessible website containing a wealth of information about drugs. It has a helpline and also social media presence where people can discuss related issues. www.talktofrank.com/

Family Lives (previously Parentline Plus) has a helpful website with advice and information about issues such as talking to teenagers about drugs. It also has a helpline for parents and carers.
www.familylives.org.uk/advice/teenagers/drugs-alcohol/

Smoking

It is not illegal for a young person to smoke, but it is illegal for someone to buy cigarettes or sell cigarettes to anyone under 18.

Many young people in care develop a smoking habit, often at a young age, which they may feel has helped them cope with depression and other difficulties in their lives. In the long run, this habit will affect their health and you have a duty as their carer to help them look at ways they can give up – but you might need to pick your time carefully, to prevent increasing stress.

Obviously nobody can make somebody else give up smoking, and nagging is unlikely to help, so look for opportunities to encourage the young person. If they moan about the cost of smoking or how far away the shop is, this may be an opportunity to start a conversation about whether they've ever thought about giving up, and how much they know about the effects, and also the support that's available to help them quit.

If they do agree to quit, then don't make too big a thing of it, put too much pressure on the young person or embarrass them in front of their friends. Just be gently encouraging and acknowledge all the achievements they make. Young people tend to be creatures of extremes so help them to understand that one lapse back into something doesn't mean they have failed. Don't let the young person slip into patterns of blaming themselves for failure, but focus on the positives – 'You managed a whole day without a smoke – which is incredible – so don't beat yourself up for one little lapse. Just keep going.'

There are many sources of support, such as nicotine replacement therapy (NRT), which is proven to have a much higher success rate than willpower alone. NHS Stop Smoking Advisers can also provide support and suggestions to manage cravings. Opinions still differ on whether vaping/e-cigarettes are definitely a healthier option in the long term, but overall any addictive habit is not going to be in the young person's best interests.

The NHS under-18s guide to quitting smoking (www.nhs.uk/live-well/quit-smoking/quitting-smoking-under-18s-guide/) contains eight reasons for giving up smoking. In addition to the usual advice about improving lung capacity, skin condition and fertility, it also includes a tool for working out how much money individuals will save if they quit. It also points out that someone who starts smoking at 15 is three times more likely to die from cancer than someone who starts smoking in their mid-20s. There is also a powerful environmental argument, as deforestation because of tobacco production accounts for nearly five per cent of overall deforestation in the developing world. The guide also includes the encouraging message that 'Two-thirds of teenagers say smoking reduces sexual attractiveness'.

Emerging sexuality and sexual health

Messages about sexuality are often very confusing for young people – and both those in and out of care can grow up with damaging ideas about sex being shameful, something to exploit for money, or a way of rebelling against society's expectations. Fostered young people may have experienced sexual abuse or exploitation, witnessed sexual activity at an early age or be especially vulnerable because of learning disabilities. Young people may also have been thrown out of home because they are lesbian, gay, bisexual, or struggling to assert their right to be transgender or of no definite gender, in an environment where this is frowned upon. As their carer, it is your role to show that you accept them as they are, value them regardless of what they've experienced, and accept the sexual/gender identity with which they have chosen to define themselves. Because if you don't accept and support them, who will?

Your task is to support them to feel comfortable and accepting of their own sexuality and to grow up aware of their rights to enjoy their bodies, while keeping themselves safe from disease, unwanted pregnancy and abusive relationships. You need to create an environment in which they feel able to ask questions, share their thoughts and enter into discussions about all matters around sex.

You also need also to be respectful of a young person's religious and cultural beliefs, which may be very different to your own. You might have very liberal views or more traditional views, possibly relating to your religious beliefs, but you owe it to the young person to help them grow up recognising that sex is a normal, healthy activity, not something to be ashamed of or brushed under the carpet.

> Your personal views are not relevant to your role in supporting the young person to talk, avoid risk and seek help and make informed decisions.

(Coleman *et al*, 2016, p20)

If you are clear about your own values, then it is easier to ensure that you don't let them affect the way in which you talk to a young person about sex and relationships. For example, you might feel that working in the sex industry is wrong, but a young person may have relatives and friends who are sex workers, and you need to respect that.

Learning about consent

One of the most valuable lessons you can teach a young person is that sexual activity should only be entered into when there is full consent from those involved. Young people can easily access pornography on the internet and this can distort their ideas of what a healthy sexual relationship looks like. Boys can feel under pressure to perform in certain ways, and girls can be browbeaten into taking part in acts they don't feel comfortable about.

The Tea and Consent video produced in 2015 by Thames Valley Police puts across an amusing and highly effective message about recognising when someone is agreeing to something and when they are not. It has been widely used in education and can be a good resource to share and discuss with young people (www.youtube.com/watch?v=pZwvrxVavnQ).

Betty Martin's Wheel of Consent work (https://bettymartin.org/videos/) is a valuable tool to help adults recognise their boundaries and learn how to say yes or no to what they want or don't want in terms of being touched by other people. It can be very empowering for all areas of life because of its strong emphasis on learning about the right to say no, and especially valuable for sharing with young people whose previous negative experiences have left them feeling disempowered or confused about their ownership of their bodies.

Safe sex

There's a lot of helpful information online about types of contraception, plus information you can pick up from your GP's surgery. You will probably want to make sure you are up to date on this before you have any conversations with young people. For example, are you aware that condoms are the only method of contraception that protects the user from both sexually transmitted infections (STIs) and pregnancy?

You may feel awkward attempting to start a conversation about this subject and it can be helpful to explain to the young person how you feel – and maybe share some anecdotes about how badly your own parents handled these conversations, or how you were left to find out these things by yourself. Sharing some of your own experiences (age-appropriately) can be a really good way of showing the young person that you aren't giving them a lecture. Help them understand that you aren't being judgemental, but want them to have happy and healthy sexual experiences and to protect themselves from unwanted pregnancy and STIs. They may feel awkward at first, but if you are as open and relaxed as possible they are more likely to talk to you if they have any questions or concerns.

Further resources

The **NHS** publishes useful information for young people, and details of how to find contraceptive services in your local area.
www.nhs.uk/live-well/sexual-health/getting-contraception/

The **Rees Centre's** website contains some helpful reports and recorded presentations on sex, rights and risk.
https://bit.ly/2MCdVtZ

The **National Autistic Society** publishes helpful materials on talking to teenagers about sex, which may also be useful for conversations with other young people who receive information differently to their peers.
www.autism.org.uk/about/communication/sex-education.aspx

The following website has useful information about sexuality and sexual health for young people with disabilities.
https://bit.ly/2FTfBig

Self-care

There is a chapter about looking after yourself at the end of this guide, but it's important to recognise that you may be affected by young people's behaviour. It can be distressing the first time a young person comes home "high", tells you they've had unprotected sex, stays out all night, or is mixing with "risky" people, but it's something that many foster carers become accustomed to managing. It is all part of caring for young people whose lives have been very troubled and difficult, and whose expectations of life may be very different to your own.

5 Mental health issues

This chapter will help you to recognise mental health issues that young people in your care may be experiencing, but also to learn about what can help in terms of treatments, behaviour management and adjustments to the environment. While many teenagers will experience some form of mental ill health, they tend to be more prevalent in young people in foster care, and can be more difficult to manage in their particular situations.

Mental health problems

Some of the more common mental health problems young people face are:

- **Depression** – this can be reflected in signs such as emotional bleakness, poor memory, permanent tiredness, sleep disruption, over-anxiety, and over- or under-eating.

- **Anxiety** – often described as having a constant "churning feeling", irregular heartbeat, light-headedness, sweating, nausea, and may include panic attacks.

- **Panic attacks** – these combine symptoms of anxiety with breathlessness and heart pain, and the person experiencing it can believe they are having a heart attack or are dying.

- **Obsessions** – which in their most extreme psychiatric form can become obsessive compulsive disorder (OCD) – these can focus on cleanliness, checking, perfectionism, fear of hurting others or throwing away something useful, or take the form of violent or "forbidden" thoughts about sex.

- **Phobias** – such as agoraphobia and claustrophobia.

If you've had robust mental health yourself, it can be hard to imagine how it feels to experience these issues. Ask the young person to explain what it's like for them, show them that you take their issues seriously and are trying to put yourself in their shoes.

In some cases, there may be a more severe mental health condition that may be affecting the young person's ability to function, such as schizophrenia, psychosis or bipolar disorder (previously referred to as manic depression). If you feel that a condition is not being recognised, talk to the young person's social worker and your supervising social worker. It will be helpful to keep detailed notes of any behaviours or signs of ill health that you observe. Ultimately, only a psychiatrist can diagnose a mental illness and they may be reluctant to put a label on a young person unless there are clear benefits to doing this.

Managing worries

There are a range of toys and gadgets on the market to help young people manage their anxieties. Worry Eaters are cute, quirky, plush characters in colours and designs which will appeal to most teenagers. Worries, fears and causes of anger can be written down and zipped into the Worry Eater's mouth, so they can be discussed later in a safe space. You will find a variety of them online, on websites such as Amazon.

Treatments

A range of different treatments are known to help young people with depression, anxiety and related mental health issues. These include talking therapies, counselling, psychoanalysis, CBT (Cognitive Behaviour Therapy – using thinking to change feelings), DBT (dialectical behaviour therapy – which combines acceptance of feelings and using thinking to change feelings), and IPT (interpersonal therapy – which puts emphasis on the symptoms of issues like grief, life-changing events, conflict and poor relationships, and has been shown to be effective for the treatment of adolescent depression).

Complementary therapies, such as mindfulness, meditation and yoga, may be beneficial in promoting relaxation and self-regulation. Equine-assisted therapy and music therapy may also be helpful. Natural therapies, such as flower essences and herbal medicines, may also prove helpful for some young people. (As a foster carer, you may also find complementary therapies useful for helping you to manage your own stress levels.)

Where possible, medical services try to avoid prescribing antidepressants to young people, because their brains are still developing. However, if the young person has not responded to therapies and/or is at high risk of suicide or self-harm, then SSRIs[1] may be prescribed. Young people with psychotic conditions may also be prescribed drugs to help manage these. For more information, visit: https://bit.ly/2Rd0BNA.

Further resources

Fursland E (2016) *The Adopter's Handbook on Therapy*, London: CoramBAAF

Living with the aftermath of trauma

Many fostered young people will have experienced trauma in their lives, which can affect their mental well-being.

Young people who have been through trauma may develop post-traumatic stress disorder (PTSD) that may be "triggered"[2] by something that brings back extremely vivid memories of the event. It can be so vivid that they believe they are actually experiencing this event again. Triggers are different for different people, and can be caused by a wide range of things, including sights, sounds, smells, dreams, reading about a similar incident, seeing a place name for somewhere they were abused, hearing a report on the TV, or even being in a room similar to one where the original trauma happened.

The young person may react in a variety of ways, which can include anger, panic, terror, depression, running away or cowering in a corner. It's essential to stay as calm as you can when a young person is triggered, and to demonstrate clearly that you believe what is happening for them. Don't try to make them talk about their experience but do listen if they need to talk about it – and they may need to do this many times over. Get them away from the triggering situation as quickly as possible. Offering them food and water or a hot drink

---

1 Selective serotonin reuptake inhibitors, a widely used form of antidepressant.

2 "Triggering" occurs when something (perhaps a sound, sight or smell) causes a negative emotional response, linked to a past trauma. Responses can include fear, sadness, panic, flashbacks, etc, and physical symptoms associated with these emotions, such as shaking, feeling faint, etc.

can be comforting, and it can help to take them out for a walk or some form of exercise, to break the sense of being stuck in the traumatic situation.

> *When a young person triggers you don't always know what to do. A therapist suggested that the best thing is to get them out, walking or doing something physical, and I've found this helpful. The change of scene seems to work for the lad I'm currently fostering and he's starting to relax when we're halfway round the park.*

(Helen, foster carer)

Dissociation

A person who has experienced a traumatic event may disconnect from their thoughts, feelings, memories or sense of identity. This often passes after a few hours, days or weeks. However, in some cases – especially when related to repeated trauma – the person can develop a dissociative disorder, for which they need professional help. The condition is often associated with prolonged sexual abuse in childhood. This is a complex area, and there is detailed information available from professional organisations such as Mind (https://bit. ly/2FKANqB).

Self-harm

It is estimated that at least one in ten young people aged 11 and upwards self-harm, and it is far more prevalent among teenagers in foster care who may have a great deal of emotional baggage to deal with.

Young people may self-harm by:

● cutting and scratching;

● burning;

● hitting themselves against objects;

● pulling out hair;

● swallowing toxic substances.

Reasons for self-harm vary from person to person, but many young people say that causing physical pain to themselves gives them an outlet for feelings they cannot express in other ways, and helps them cope.

How to recognise if a young person is self-harming

- The young person is secretive and spends large amounts of time alone (although this is not uncommon in teenagers).

- Unexplained cuts, bruises, or cigarette burns.

- Supplies of bandages and first aid equipment in the house are being depleted.

- The young person covers themselves up – with things like long-sleeved clothing in summer.

- There may be signs of depression or low mood.

When supporting a young person who self-harms, it's important not to overreact. Focus on the young person's feelings rather than trying to get them to talk about why or how they self-harm. Do not make the young person promise not to do it again, otherwise they may not seek your help in future if they feel they have let you down.

If this is a new problem or the behaviour is getting worse, you will need to discuss it with the young person's social worker and make sure they receive support from relevant mental health services, such as CAMHS and talking therapies. Make sure you have an agreed risk management plan signed off by the young person's social worker and your supervising social worker. Focus on helping the young person to identify and express their emotions in other ways.

At the hospital when I was getting my cuts sewn up, this nurse treated me like I was dirt...like I was wasting their time 'cos I'd done it myself. My foster carer wasn't having none of that...she made me feel like I was OK and that the staff were wrong to be like that.

(Carlie, aged 17)

It is common for young people who self-harm to say that releasing pain in this way stops them from feeling suicidal, and for many that may be the case. However, at least half of all people who kill themselves have a history of self-harm, so if you have any serious concerns then it is always best to seek urgent professional help.

Nurturing young people

Young people – however tough they seem – may really welcome the opportunity to experience the comforts and care that children from healthy family situations experienced with their parents at a younger age. A scented bubble bath, fluffy towels, a hand massage with aromatherapy oils, a snuggly onesie, or cuddling up under their duvet with a teddy bear and a mug of hot chocolate can be very soothing for a distressed young person. If they dismiss all of this as childish, then look for other ways to help them feel nurtured. You could make your own sitting room cosy with nightlights and scented candles, have comfortable cushions and beanbags, and offer them the opportunity to curl up under a fleece while watching TV. Show them that it's natural and healthy for adults to enjoy some self-nurturing.

Further resources

Jackson C (2012) *Parenting a Child with Mental Health Issues*, London: BAAF

Dr Robin F Goodman, 'How to deal with a depressed teen', www.youtube.com/watch?v=3wnjyPJaV3c

6 Managing behaviour

When a young person's behaviour is challenging, it can be easy to take it personally and wonder if you're doing something wrong. Remember that the young person is managing as best they can, and their behaviour isn't about you – even if it sometimes feels like it. They are dealing with the impact on their brain and emotional development of their early experiences. They may also have additional disabilities and conditions that make processing experiences hard for them. They are trying to make sense of a world that may be full of fear and uncertainty, without the advantages of the coping mechanisms that more securely attached young people have developed. It is going to take a lot of work from you and the young person to help them learn new ways of being in the world – but it's a deeply rewarding process to help a young person learn new ways of managing their feelings.

> Adults need to practise "not startling the horses" when working with traumatised children, for children, like horses, are flight animals. Unfortunately many hyperaroused children appear anything but timid, and this leads people to treat them as frightening rather than frightened. The counter-intuitive technique is to assume with any challenging child that fear is a large part of the equation for the child, and at the same time to recognise that this will engender fear in the adult. So we must contain and manage our own fear and soothe the terror of the child.

(Cairns and Stanway, 2013)

As in other aspects of foster care, you need to make sure that you are getting plenty of support and to be aware of the impact of the young person's behaviour on other members of your family. It is much better to ask your supervising social worker for additional training, advice or just a chance to air your feelings, at an early stage, than to let a situation get to a stage where you feel you can no longer manage it.

Some helpful approaches

These are some of the approaches that are widely used in the UK for helping to manage behaviour, and helping young people to develop new ways of expressing their emotions and feeling secure.

PACE

PACE is an approach created by clinical psychologist, Dr Dan Hughes, based on his extensive work with children and young people who have experienced trauma and attachment difficulties. PACE stands for Playfulness, Acceptance, Curiosity and Empathy.

Explaining PACE, in *Parenting a Child with Emotional and Behavioural Difficulties* (2012, p25), Hughes writes:

Playfulness – conveys a state of active enjoyment when with another person. This state is easier for many abused children to experience than is affection. It conveys a sense of lightness and hope: the conflict or problem behaviour is not too big for us to manage. We will get through this together.

Acceptance – conveys a sense that you accept your child, although you may evaluate her behaviour...If her inner life is accepted and then met with an open and engaged response of empathy and curiosity, it is much more likely to change than if it is met with anger and shame-inducing comments.

Curiosity – is a non-knowing and non-judgemental stance towards your child's inner life...You are fascinated with who she is. You are gazing underneath your child's behaviour in order to better understand it...Curiosity is not: 'Why did you do that?'...Curiosity is: 'I wonder why you did that? Any ideas?'

Empathy – refers to you staying with your child in her emotional state and experiencing it with her. Through empathy, you are conveying that you deeply understand her emotions and that you are supporting and comforting her over the stress that she is feeling...Skipping empathy and moving right into giving advice and problem-solving is likely to create a defensive state in your child so that she is less likely to be open to your guidance.

The Secure Base Model

Secure Base is a model of providing care in fostering and adoption that is based on theories of attachment and resilience while also drawing on child placement research.

Gillian Schofield and Mary Beek, who developed this approach, describe five "caregiving dimensions" that provide the necessary sense of security, confidence, competence and resilience. In relation to teenagers, these caregiving dimensions support various essential aspects of the young person's developmental and emotional needs.

- **Availability** – as a foster carer of a teenager, it's not possible to be physically available all the time but the young person needs to know that you are still thinking about them and will be there for them when they return from school, from time with friends or meetings with birth relatives. This enables the young person to build trust and seek comfort from other people appropriately, discriminate between familiar people and strangers, trust people outside the family appropriately, while also becoming increasingly independent.

- **Sensitivity** – helping young people to express emotions without being overwhelmed by them, and to be able to reflect on their own feelings and behaviour and have constructive strategies for managing these.

- **Acceptance** – helping the young person to develop positive self-esteem while accepting that they can't be good at everything. It is also about having a sense of purpose, getting pleasure and satisfaction from activities, having pride in themselves, and resilience to recover from setbacks.

- **Co-operation** – helping the young person to develop the ability to get their needs met, to assert themselves appropriately, to make appropriate choices, and co-operate with parents, authority figures and peers.

- **Family membership** – helping the young person to create a sense of belonging, and to see themselves as part of the foster family.

Further resources

Schofield G and Beek M (2014) *Promoting Attachment and Resilience: A guide for foster carers and adopters on using the Secure Base model*, London: BAAF

Schofield G and Beek M (2018) *The Attachment Handbook for Foster Care and Adoption* (2nd edn), London: CoramBAAF

Providing A Secure Base website: www.uea.ac.uk/providingasecurebase/the-secure-base-model

Allowing for flexibility

During your foster carer training, you may have had experience of these models or something similar. You might find what has worked very well for several young people may not work for all young people – possibly because of the way in which some conditions (such as FASD, autism or ADHD) affect the way in which a young person processes information. If you feel that a model really isn't working for a young person (after you've tried it out for a while), or you find that there are helpful aspects from other approaches, then discuss this with your supervising social worker. Some experienced foster carers use a range of approaches, adapting these to the needs of the different young people who live with them.

Aims of behaviour management

Generally, these are the key things you are trying to achieve when you work with a young person.

- Help the young person to internalise that they are still valued and accepted, even when you don't like their behaviour and are disappointed or displeased.

- Model good self-management of feelings and behaviour for the young person. You may feel anxious inside but you need to act with calm and self-regulation so the young person can start to internalise this for themselves.

- Help the young person to make connections between inner feelings and the way they behave, for example, by speaking about your own inner processes and how these translate into your actions.

- If you are caring for a young person with a condition that means they process information differently from their peers (e.g. FASD, autism or ADHD), it can be especially helpful to put emphasis on creating structure, limiting distractions, breaking tasks into manageable pieces, and encouraging the young person to think through their feelings and behaviour out loud with you.

- Notice and communicate your awareness of the efforts and progress the young person makes in managing their behaviour. Some young people find it really hard to accept praise, so try to use specific examples of what they did well, and find times when the young person is available to receive these. 'I noticed that you calmed yourself down so quickly. I could see you were upset but you managed it well...'.

- Remember that many looked after young people carry a great deal of shame because of an internalised sense of worthlessness which can be created by difficult early experiences. (Shame is highly negative and different from guilt – guilt can be a healthy feeling that spurs the young person on to make amends and change their behaviour.) Don't be surprised if they find it hard to take even the gentlest criticism or react disproportionately to your attempts to impose boundaries or penalties for breaking rules.

- Be clear with young people about boundaries, but be prepared to be flexible and compassionate. Sometimes building the young person's sense of being accepted and cared for is more important that enforcing a rule. If you explain the reasoning behind your decisions, this can help young people to realise that it is mature to consider new options and change your mind, where appropriate.

- Show young people that you are prepared to apologise if you have lost your cool, made a mistake, or have misunderstood or wronged them in some way.

- Be careful about the way in which you think and speak about the young person's behaviour. Avoid using words like "impossible" or "nightmarish", because our brains can subconsciously believe those words and respond accordingly.

- Be aware of your own values and beliefs and recognise that these may be very different to those of the young person. Be clear about where you are able to be flexible and where you are not able to compromise your own values.

- Find out, if you can, how the young person sees their life experiences and how this affects their feelings and behaviour.

- Deep listening shows that you really care enough to hear what the young person wants to tell you, but also what they don't say. This can tell you a great deal about how they are feeling, not how you *think* they are feeling.

- Remember that surprises and treats can be alarming for a young person who cannot distinguish between fear and excitement.

- A young person's challenging behaviour may escalate before something pleasant is about to happen. This is because the young person is unable to believe that good things can happen and that they are worthy of these – so they will sabotage the situation rather than risk disappointment.

- Pick your battles carefully. Be prepared to let go of some of the minor issues that you might enforce with your own children, because there will be much bigger issues to resolve for this young person.

- Don't let other people's responses affect you. They might not let their teenager do X or Y in the supermarket, but they have no idea how much the young person you are caring for has been through, and how much their behaviour has improved since they came to live with you.

- When a young person has misbehaved or lost control of their emotions, it can be counterproductive to send them away. Being abandoned or rejected was something they probably experienced a lot in abusive situations. They may need your presence to help them calm themselves.

- Recognise that some young people will want time and space on their own to calm down and reflect, and allow them this if it is their preference.

- See each young person as an individual. Trends in behaviour management techniques change, and if you have a particular young person who has responded really well to a particular approach in the past, it may be unwise to change it unless there is a good reason for doing so.

- Be consistent. And keep going. If you've tried everything and the young person isn't responding, then don't give up. If you show that you don't care what the young person does, then you are not offering them appropriate support. Keep trying – and take good care of yourself (see the chapter on self-care for foster carers).

There are days when you feel nothing goes right and whatever you do the young person doesn't respond. And that is really hard, but you can't give up. It's tempting to say, 'Oh, just do what you want then', but then you're giving up on the young person. Because that young person needs to know you do care, and you're doing your best for them...and maybe somewhere down the line they'll be one of the ones who comes back in the future and says, 'You remember when you used to keep telling me you knew I had it in me? Well, I think about that sometimes, and it keeps me going.'

(Fran, foster carer)

If you can recognise what lies behind a young person's behaviour, then you can help them to start getting their needs met in more appropriate ways. You can do this by acknowledging that you recognise their feelings may be causing them distress. The phrase 'I imagine' can be very helpful – for example, 'I imagine it must be hard leaving behind the friends from your old school...'

Using consequences

Some parenting approaches rely on consequences, and there is an evidence base for behavioural social learning approaches, for example, Multidimensional Treatment Foster Care, or Fostering Changes. The skill for many foster carers is to manage behaviour – including consequences – while maintaining a good relationship with the young person.

Using consequences – such as: 'If you don't do this then you won't get that', or: 'If you do that again, you won't be allowed to come out with us' – with a young person who has insecure attachments can be ineffective, even counterproductive. The young person may want to deliberately defy you in order to upset or anger you, or to reinforce their belief that all adults will ultimately reject them. Also, what you see as a "treat" may be something the young person sees as alarming (because they can't distinguish between exciting and frightening), and they're looking for a way to get out of it. There may be all sorts of reasons behind their behaviour that you don't understand, and by using sanctions you can make the situation worse rather than helping them to manage their behaviour.

You need to think carefully before using sanctions with young people, and to base this on what you know about the feelings and history that lie behind their behaviour. Just because sanctions have worked well with one young person does not mean they will be effective with another.

> *We have fostered our two girls for quite a long time, and the older one has responded to the idea that if she keeps her part of the bargain and does X, Y and Z during the day without kicking off, then she gets her phone and internet access in the evening. But the younger girl doesn't think and react the same way. She has many of the signs of foetal alcohol spectrum disorder and she just doesn't get the idea of not being allowed her phone if she doesn't keep her side of the bargain. Her brain just doesn't work that way and her challenging behaviour escalates if you try to use any kind of sanction with her.*

(Renée, foster carer)

If the emphasis is on promoting the attachment between you and the young person, then you may want to minimise the consequences of a young person's behaviour – as severe sanctions could damage the connections you are building. However, in some cases your agreed role as a foster carer may be to help the young person function in a socially acceptable way – and in these situations using consequences may be the most effective way to achieve this.

> *We were fostering a boy with learning difficulties and what worked well for him was lots of structure. His day was mapped out with pictures of clocks and it was all about 'If you want to do this, then you need to do that'. His relationship with us wasn't part of the way he viewed the world. He was able to move from being restrained every day to being able to move around by himself. But that approach wouldn't work for the vast majority of fostered children.*

(Karl, foster carer)

Further resources

Pallett C *et al* (2015) *Managing Difficult Behaviour: How to improve relationships*, London: CoramBAAF

Non-violent resistance (NVR)

If a young person is violent towards you or other people in your family, it can be very distressing. It's all too easy to start thinking, 'I should be able to control this behaviour', and wondering what you are doing wrong. This can be counterproductive because you are more likely to escalate the situation as the young person picks up on and reacts to your behaviour.

> *When a child is violent and aggressive, parents often use a strategy that attempts to control the child's behaviour, but most children respond by refusing to be controlled.*

(Fursland, 2016)

The principle behind NVR is that attempting to control the young person's behaviour can intensify the confrontation. It recommends that carers focus on de-escalating the situation.

- Make it clear that the young person's behaviour is unacceptable, but that you do not intend to use any form of aggressive words or behaviour yourself, and that you are not getting into a power struggle.

- Let go of any desire you have to stay in control of the young person's behaviour. In this situation, you can only control yourself but not the young person.

- Focus on minimising risk and protecting yourself and anyone else in the situation.

- Get the help of anyone who can act as mediators and supporters – to act as "witnesses" so that the young person knows their behaviour isn't being kept secret.

- Use "parental presence" to modify the young person's behaviour, for example, staging a "sit-in" in the young person's room until they make a constructive suggestion.

- Be ready to take steps towards reconciliation, such as making the young person a cup of tea or suggesting an activity with them.

NVR may be delivered as a course or a therapy. If you are having problems managing violent behaviour, ask your supervising social worker about this, if it has not already been offered to you.

It is also important to know and respect your limits – and the limits of other members of your household (this may include other fostered children), and be prepared to seek help.

Further resources

Partnership Projects, an organisation that offers workshops, training and consultancy in various therapies, provides training in NVR. www.partnershipprojectsuk.com/non-violent-resistance-nvr/introduction-to-nvr/

Keeping yourself calm

As a foster carer, you are human – and it's only natural that there will be times when you feel deeply frustrated. Young people will easily pick up on this and you need to demonstrate calmness, in order to prevent the young person's behaviour from escalating and to model effective ways of managing feelings.

> *You need to react in a calm and measured way, be mindful and attuned. I use all the techniques I've learnt for reprogramming myself – breathing deeply, use my anchors to remind myself of calm, soothing places – so I'm not responding to my blood pressure starting to rise. So I'm not mirroring their increasing emotions as they hit their head against the wall, throw things or threaten me...You have to feel in control, you can't go around wondering how you will cope because the young people will pick up on that. Young people will make every attempt to get you to reject them. They can bait you to hit them, because that's what adults have always done to them before. They seek the triggers to keep that cycle in place. All that deep-seated developmental and fractured attachment takes a long time to come to terms with...they are unable to process things...So you have to be calm, and keep getting calmer.*

(Sian, experienced foster carer)

This does not mean that you can never show your emotions – sometimes a young person needs to know that you are angry or upset.

> *Sometimes being angry when your child does something that seems outrageous may be necessary and the most appropriate response. If she kicks the dog, she may need to see that you are angry about that behaviour*

in order to appreciate how serious it was. If you save your anger for such major incidents, not routine misbehaviour, she is likely to benefit from it in those instances. And if you repair your relationship as soon as possible after the expression of anger, she is likely to feel guilt over her behaviour, rather than shame.

(Hughes, 2012, p47)

Modelling resilience

Naturally, you want to handle young people's behaviour to the best of your ability, but making mistakes can have its positive side. Young people are bound to make mistakes themselves, and it can be very helpful for them to see that you too make mistakes, but aren't afraid to acknowledge them, and don't give up. Learning about resilience is a helpful lesson for looked after young people whose previous lives may have led them to feel that nothing will ever improve. Your "stickability" can also create an atmosphere in which the young person recognises that you are less likely to give up on them, which can help them start to learn about trust.

Further resources

Cairns K and Cairns B (2016) *Attachment, Trauma and Resilience*, London: CoramBAAF

Hughes D (2013) *Parenting a Child with Emotional and Behavioural Difficulties*, London: BAAF

Golding K (2008) *Nurturing Attachments: Supporting children who are fostered or adopted,* London: Jessica Kingsley Publishers

Sunderland M (2012) *Helping Teenagers with Anger and Low Self-Esteem*, Banbury: Hinton House

7 Supporting education

Young people in care may have widely varying experiences of school. For some, it may represent a place of refuge where they distracted themselves from the pressures or memories of home life, where they have friends and connections, and feel able to fulfil their potential. For others, it will be a place where they feel disengaged, unwanted and misunderstood, and where they are unlikely to achieve very much. Multiple school moves and disruptive experiences in their early life may have left them behind their peer group in their learning. As their carer, you can play an important role in providing the stability and support to help the young person feel more secure at school.

You can also help the school to recognise and respond to the needs of the young person in more appropriate ways. Increasingly, schools are recognising that young people with attachment issues need different approaches to their peers, but some schools still fail to recognise these issues and can use conventional teaching approaches with young people who are unlikely to respond to them.

The support structure in schools

Each school should have a designated teacher with specific responsibility for looked after children. In secondary school, some of this responsibility may be delegated to the head of year/head of achievement or the head of pastoral care. For young people with special educational needs, there may also be a SENCO or head of inclusion, and/or a teaching assistant and learning mentor with special responsibility for the young person.

In England, there will also be a virtual team for looked after children, with a virtual head, who champions the educational needs of the local authority's looked after children, whether or not they are living within its geographical area. Virtual heads should be able to help you with issues such as finding the most appropriate school for a young person, and preventing exclusions. Your local authority will also have an educational team for looked after children and a head of inclusion.

Educational structures and staff titles can vary from school to school and authority to authority. You can't be expected to know all of these, so simply ask which member of staff covers the area you have concerns or questions about.

All children and young people in care in England and Wales should have a Personal Education Plan (PEP), which should be completed by their social worker in conjunction with the young person, the designated teacher at the school, parents or relevant family members, any other agency (possibly a member of the virtual school team), and you, as the foster carer.

If the young person's educational needs are not being met, you can request an Educational, Health and Care review (EHC) (in England), or a review for an Individual Development Plan (IDP) (in Wales), or a review for a Co-ordinated Support Plan (CSP) in Scotland.

Further resources

Alix S (2019, forthcoming) *The Foster Carer's Handbook on Education*, London: CoramBAAF

Fursland E with Cairns K and Stanway C (2013) *Ten Top Tips on Supporting Education*, London: BAAF

Fursland E (2018) *The Adopter's Handbook on Education*, London: CoramBAAF

The **Child Law Advice** website has a useful section about the educational entitlements of looked after children.
https://bit.ly/2HyHXjq

Conditions that may affect young people's learning process

In addition to behavioural issues or developmental conditions, young people may also experience learning difficulties that impact on their experience at school.

Dyslexia

Some of the symptoms seen in teenagers are:

- problems with reading, spelling and reading aloud;
- problems in engaging with a story on the page, which they may not experience when listening or watching the story in another form;
- trouble with expressions that are not literal;
- difficulty with time management;
- problems learning a new language.

Dyspraxia

Dyspraxia, a form of developmental coordination disorder (DCD), is a common disorder affecting fine and/or gross motor co-ordination in children and adults. It may also affect speech. DCD is a lifelong condition, formally recognised by international organisations including the World Health Organisation. An individual's co-ordination difficulties may affect participation and functioning of everyday life skills in education, work and employment.

(Dyspraxia Foundation: https://dyspraxiafoundation.org.uk/about-dyspraxia/)

Your role as a foster carer

You can play a valuable role in ensuring that the young person's education plan reflects their personality and needs, and then ensuring that it is effectively implemented. You may see a very different side to the young person at home to that presented in school, and be more aware than their teachers of their strengths and challenges, hobbies and personal interests. You may also be aware whether there are existing issues for the young person in their current school or any school being considered for them, for example, you may know about bullying within the school; people who are important to the young person, such as a member of catering staff who has always looked out for them; and about the positive and negative influences of friends and even gang members who the young person may come across in a particular neighbourhood. You are also likely to be aware if the young person has any birth relatives in the school. Being in the same school as a sibling can be a very positive experience for a young person, but being in the same environment as an extended family member who has contact with someone who has abused or threatened the young person could cause them huge distress.

Once the plan is in place, you can play an important role in observing how it is impacting on the young person's life and noticing what is working and what isn't.

Some points to bear in mind

- Discuss with the young person how much of their personal history they want to share with schoolmates, and model answers that they can give to questions about their home life.

- Information should be shared on a need-to-know basis with teachers and educational staff, and there can be advantages in certain teachers understanding more about the difficulties that a young person has faced, or what triggers them.

- Try to ensure that the young person isn't taken out of lessons for meetings or specialist appointments, because this can draw attention to them and lead to questions or teasing from other young people.

- Encourage out-of-school activities where a young person can develop and recognise talents and interests. This can help improve their resilience and self-esteem if they are struggling academically, but also creates a more "rounded" individual, and can significantly improve the young person's chance of a satisfying adult life.

- Ensure that your fostered young person gets as much preparation and support as possible for transitions – not just moves to new schools, but also moves to new school years, new teachers and new buildings can be challenging for some young people who have had experiences of separation and loss.

How aware is the school of attachment issues and difficulties faced by young people in care?

Louise Michelle Bomber, writing about pupils with attachment issues, states that for a young person with an already fragmented sense of self, multiple transitions can be very harmful, if not handled well. She writes that such young people can easily be left behind, misunderstood and possibly excluded. Bomber believes that we must "overcompensate" for everything young people have missed out on in their earlier lives, and not just hope that young people will settle down and get on with their learning by themselves. Schools, she suggests, must actively create an environment that provides for fostered young people's particular needs.

> These young people need someone and somewhere that can demonstrate that they are being "kept in mind" during their numerous transitions. Someone who can hold everything together for them. Somewhere familiar they can return to. With this emotional scaffolding in place, the young person is more likely to have the confidence, courage and curiosity to explore and attempt new tasks and learning, out in the wider context of school. This relationship needs to be built upon and strengthened throughout the school year.
>
> (Bomber, 2009, p41)

Bomber suggests that there are a variety of ways in which schools can provide this "emotional scaffolding" (you will, no doubt, recognise in her recommendations many of the elements you are attempting to create for the young person at home):

- A safe physical space in the school with familiar faces which the young person can return to – perhaps in the inclusion unit if the school has this. It can be helpful if the young person can go to this space at the beginning of the day, be warmly greeted and "grounded" for the day ahead.

- A key adult/member of staff in the school who is physically and emotionally available – not just a name on a piece of paper. Ideally, the young person should be involved in choosing this person.

- Ensuring that the young person's file arrives before the young person moves schools, and is read by the appropriate people (with a caveat about confidentiality). Staff may worry about "prejudging" young people, but Bomber argues that it is better to do this than overlook or misjudge a young person's needs.

- Making endings a positive experience for the young person. Even if things have gone wrong, the young person needs time to say goodbyes and to learn from the experience. 'This may be the first time in the young person's life that a fraught ending has been handled by mature adults, so we need to make the most of the possibility of giving them a different experience of what life can be like' (Bomber, 2009, p46).

- Ensuring that the young person doesn't get overwhelmed, and has support from the key adult in managing the school timetable, any additional support they receive, and that the number of adults involved and changes of space are kept as low as possible.

Your young person may be lucky enough to attend a school that has awareness of the impact of attachment disorders and other conditions affecting looked after young people, or you may be able to work with the child's social worker and other relevant staff (such as the head of the virtual school) to find a school that has greater commitment to the needs of your teenager. Even if the school has a commitment to supporting looked after young people, individual teachers may have their own prejudices about the "type" of children who come into care, and have little or no experience of dealing with children affected by trauma, hyperarousal, diminished impulse control, or dissociation from their feelings and emotions.

Teachers may feel defensive if they think you are critical of the way in which they have handled a situation, so try to be as open and friendly as possible (however frustrated you may feel). Perhaps you could share some of the behaviour issues you have found surprising or challenging as a foster carer (whilst preserving confidentiality), and what you've learnt from these, to create a sense of rapport with the teacher.

You can also ask for support from the child's social worker, the designated teacher, or the special educational needs co-ordinator (SENCO), or a member of the virtual school team.

Even in schools that can't provide the level of resources Bomber recommends, a staff member who is aware of the young person's need for a safe space and a consistent person to talk to can provide helpful support. This person may be able to find ways in which to meet the young person's needs, and to limit the number of classroom changes and people the young person has to deal with.

Further resources

Bomber LM (2011) *What about Me? Inclusive strategies to support pupils with attachment difficulties make it through the school day*, London: Worth Publishing

Bomber LM (2016) *Attachment Aware School Series* (box set of five pocket books), London: Worth Publishing

Encouraging and supporting the learning process

Even if your own experience of education wasn't particularly positive and you sometimes find it difficult to be encouraging, there are various ways in which you can help the young person to get the best out of their time at school. There are many resources online that explain issues such as the amount of homework given at various stages, and suggestions for activities to support education, such as encouraging the young person to watch the news and read a newspaper, and looking out for stories that relate to topics they're covering in school.

The BBC website Bitesize section has lots of information to help you keep abreast of the educational system, learning expectations and resources that you can use with young people: www.bbc.com/bitesize/learn.

There are also some great suggestions online for encouraging young people to read, for example, the Parentzone Scotland Supporting Literacy at Home website has a downloadable leaflet for secondary education, and a film clip, 'Video 5: Secondary – age 12 to 16', which explains that teenagers, who are less likely to be interested in fiction, may be more drawn to books that reflect their interests, e.g. a biography about a comedian or sportsperson they admire (https://bit.ly/2Mz7qrV).

If you feel unsure about your own literacy or numeracy skills, or English is not your first language and you do not feel very confident in advising a young person on these subjects, there are a number of resources to help you improve your own skills and knowledge. Again, the BBC has very accessible online resources at: www.bbc.co.uk/skillswise/learners.

You can also support your teenager by studying yourself. In *Ten Top Tips for Supporting Education*, Eileen Fursland writes:

Some children who struggle to concentrate on homework will find it much easier if they can work alongside someone else at the kitchen table, for instance.

Carers who are themselves continuing to learn are excellent role models, and it hardly matters what they are learning, whether it's cake decorating, football refereeing, playing the guitar, dance classes or computer literacy. Any interest the carer shows in studying, taking classes or developing their own skills demonstrates to the child the pleasure of learning and improving.

(2013, p42)

New opportunities

At the time this book went to press, a new scheme had been launched by the Government to create mentoring and scholarship schemes for looked after children in England, through partnerships with independent schools. More information can be found here: https://bit.ly/2TdV4YR.

Higher and further education

Information about this is included in the following chapter.

8 Preparation for leaving care

Under legislation such as Staying Put in England and Scotland, and When I am Ready in Wales, fostered young people can opt to stay with their foster carers beyond the age of 18, usually up to the age of 21, or 25 if they are in higher education. This can be a great solution for the young person, but depends on whether you, as the foster carer, are prepared to offer this. You will need to consider your family's personal and financial circumstances and other children whom you may be fostering. Your supervising social worker will be able to tell you more about this.

Creating positive futures

Making the transition to adult life can be daunting for most young people, but for young people in foster care it can feel very frightening. As a foster carer, part of your role is to help the young person prepare for their future. You need to do everything in your power to make sure the young person is as ready as they can possibly be to enjoy a rounded and satisfying life. Supporting them to attain educationally is very important, but so is teaching them the skills they will need to negotiate life's ups and downs, and the attitudes that will make them open to new interests, to making friends and being able to enjoy small successes and small pleasures, as well as the larger ones.

It can be helpful to make yourself aware of what a young person is entitled to in terms of statutory support, and to support the young person to find out for themselves. There is a range of information available online, for example, the Children's Commissioner for England website has a dedicated section: www.childrenscommissioner.gov.uk/help-at-hand/leaving-care-your-rights/. The Children and Young People's Commissioner Scotland has information here: https://www.cypcs.org.uk/rights/your-rights-to-care; and information can also be found on the Children's Commissioner for Wales website here: www.childcomwales.org.uk/.

Personal Assistants and Pathway Plans

Typically, young people in foster care are entitled to an assessment of their needs, to leave foster care at a time that feels right for them, and to remain in foster care if they choose to do so, up to a certain age. The young person's wishes and views should form the basis of their personal Pathway Plan. All young people leaving care should have a Pathway Plan and it is the duty of their social worker to make sure that they have a Personal Assistant (PA) to support them with this.

Every young person in care should have a PA who helps them plan towards their adult life and ensures that when they leave care they are provided with appropriate support. There are no official qualifications for a PA but this person is likely to be a social worker or a specialist leaving care worker, or someone working in careers and training. It is good practice for a young person to have the same PA throughout their time in care and up until they are 21 or 25 (depending on their situation).

Pathway Plans should cover the following areas of the young person's life:

- Health

- Education, training and employment

- Identity

- Family and social relationships

- Emotional and behavioural development

- Self-care skills and social presentation

- Finance

- Support

- Family and environmental factors

- Accommodation

Each young person will have different needs and some may find it reassuring to start work on their Pathways Plans at an earlier age, while others will find it unsettling to begin so soon. Young people with learning disabilities should not be overlooked in this process – they are as much entitled to their own PA and Pathway Plan as anyone else. Additional support should be made available if the young person has communication needs or learning disabilities, in order to help them express their wishes and opinions.

Your role

As the young person's carer, you should be one of the people consulted as part of this process, and you have an important role to play in ensuring that the young person you are fostering has a truly effective Pathway Plan. For example, you could be the one to recognise that when the young person speaks about their hopes to work in a café in the future, this does not mean that they want to follow a career in catering, but that they like the idea of meeting with members of the public and would probably be more interested in hospitality. Don't be afraid to challenge anything in the Pathway Plan that you feel does not reflect the young person as you know them. It is unproductive for a young person to be forced into a line of training just because their worker misunderstood their interests.

Pathway Plans are meant to ensure that the young person's needs are not overlooked and should never be considered as "written in stone". You can encourage the young person to review their decisions as their interests change.

Be ambitious for the young person and encourage them to fulfil their potential. Find out as much as you can about how the academic system works, when exams take place, what qualifications are needed for entry to higher or further education, any changes in legislation, or introductions of new schemes. Many young people will say that they would prefer to go to college after school because they are attracted to the idea of more freedom, but some will struggle with the less structured college environment. Make sure that they are aware of the options available to them, and encourage them to make use of career services at school, online information and any talks or presentations about educational and career opportunities.

Support young people to develop skills

Help young people to develop the skills they will need to manage their lives as young adults, and to increase their chances of succeeding to the best of their ability in education, training and employment. This includes everyday skills such as budgeting, shopping, washing, cleaning and personal hygiene, but also personal skills (sometimes called "soft skills"), such as creating rapport with people they meet, negotiation, how to contact public services, learning how to approach people in positions of authority, how to query mistakes and complain effectively (but politely), how to apologise if they themselves make a mistake, and how to be resilient when things go wrong.

Further resources

The **British Council** website has an interesting article on teaching "soft skills" to young people.
https://bit.ly/2hlvTQ1

Coram Voice provides information and advice about a wide range of issues for young people in care and leaving care, including on advocacy, rights and entitlements, making complaints, and online safety.
https://coramvoice.org.uk/

Bond H (2008) *Ten Top Tips for Preparing Care Leavers*, London: BAAF

The overall situation

There is a legal requirement for young people between the ages of 16–18 to be in education, employment or training. More information about this can be found at: www.bbc.co.uk/schools/parents/education_after_16/. You may also hear the term NEET being used (refers to young people who are not in education, employment or training).

For young people in care, this can be much more complicated than for those living with their families, because the issue of where they will be living is central. They may still be living with you under Staying Put legislation in England and Scotland, or Am I Ready? in Wales, if you, your family and the young person are happy with this.

If the young person does not continue to live with you, their PA has to help them find alternative accommodation, such as semi-independent living offered by a voluntary sector or private provider. If they are considered independent enough, they may be eligible to apply for council accommodation. The amount of financial support available varies according to age and circumstances.

The Care Leavers' Association has a range of information about the available entitlements and opportunities for care leavers: www.careleavers.com/what-we-do/young-peoples-project/.

The Scottish Care Leavers Covenant was created by an alliance of stakeholders with the aim of closing the gap between policy and practice for care leavers. Local authorities, voluntary sector organisations and companies are asked to commit to support care leavers in areas such as health, housing, training and employment. Some authorities have, for example, signed up to making care leavers exempt from council tax. For more information, visit: https://bit.ly/2sHDYaa.

Benefits and grants

There is a lot of information online about benefits and grants for care leavers. This includes the following examples, but an online search will find many more.

- **Buttle UK** provides grants and some support to young people who are estranged from their families: www.buttleuk.org/need-support/young-people#help

- The **Rees Foundation** can sometimes help with financial grants: http://dev.reesfoundation.org/contact/

- Organisations such as the **Care Leavers Foundation** make small grants to care leavers aged over 21 (and usually up to about the age of 26): www.thecareleaversfoundation.org/about_grants

- **Shelter Scotland** publishes useful information about benefits, grants and support for care leavers: https://bit.ly/2SbaZK0

Further and higher education

Together with the Virtual School and your young person's PA, you can support and encourage them to find out about the options open for them in further and higher education. Ideally, the young person will get fully involved in this but parents can find that their own children get overwhelmed and seem demotivated when thinking about their future, so it's not surprising that looked after young people – whose futures can feel very uncertain – may need a lot of practical support at this stage.

In recent years, universities have made concerted efforts to encourage and support young people from care, and while this won't be appropriate for every young person, don't hesitate to encourage the young person you care for to consider university as a possibility.

To find out what individual universities offer, it's best to contact them directly, but students should also tick the "care leavers" box on the UCAS form so that their chosen universities and colleges can let them know what additional support they are entitled to. This could include help with finances such as Higher Education Bursaries, or awards and grants from certain organisations such as the Rees Foundation (www.reesfoundation.org/), and the Unite Foundation Scholarship Scheme, which offers accommodation costs in partnership with 10 universities for students in London (www.unitefoundation. co.uk/get-a-scholarship/), or additional support provided on campus or by an external organisation. A number of colleges and universities have developed schemes where students can continue to live on campus all year round, rather than being expected to find accommodation during holidays.

Further information can be found at www.ucas.com/undergraduate/applying-university/individual-needs/ucas-undergraduate-support-care-leavers

Further education (FE) refers to education that is additional to that received at secondary school, such as A Levels, vocational programmes, technical colleges and adult education retraining.

Higher education (HE) refers to education offered in universities and institutes of higher education – at undergraduate and postgraduate level. However, not everyone understands these distinctions and you will see blurring of the categories on some websites and employer application forms.

The following examples are some of the FE and HE options available for looked after young people.

- The **UCAS** toolkit for care leavers offers a wide range of information about A Levels, BTECs, NVQs, career ideas, apprenticeships for post-16s, finance, and local funding: www.ucas.com/advisers/toolkits/supporting-care-leavers-toolkit

- The **Propel** website is run by Become, the charity for children in care and young care leavers. It covers the whole of the UK and has a range of information about courses, funding and financial support, including for asylum-seeking young people: https://propel.org.uk/uk/support/

- In Northern Ireland, the website *Pathways to Further and Higher Education for Looked After and Care Experienced Young People* offers a wealth of useful information: https://bit.ly/2DyUKyc

- The **National Network for the Education of Care Leavers** (NNECL) has helpful information about FE and HE, including introduction days at universities, summer schools, conferences, information about distance learning and CPD. They also have a range of helpful videos, for example, showing what university accommodation looks like: http://www.nnecl.org/

- The information below is taken from **Fostering Network's** website section, 'Talking about higher education and the future': https://bit.ly/2UewTcJ

We encourage young people who have spent time in care to Tick the Box on their UCAS form saying they are care experienced (www. thefosteringnetwork.org.uk/get-involved/our-campaigns/tick-box); this is confidential but will ensure they get the extra support they are entitled to while at university – this could include bursaries, year-round accommodation and study support.

(Social worker)

Training and apprenticeships

Virtual schools (see Chapter 7) are expected to make information available about education, employment and training opportunities for young people and many will have direct links with these schemes. A number of local authorities have created in-house apprenticeship schemes and some even have pre-apprenticeships for those who are not ready for a full apprenticeship. There are also some national schemes to provide support for young people in care or leaving care. The following are examples of schemes which are current at the time of publication.

- The **Care Leaver Covenant England** is a promise made by private, public or voluntary organisations to provide support for care leavers aged 16–25 in England to help them to live independently. More than 50 businesses, charities and every government department in England have signed up to the Covenant, which commits to provide work-based opportunities to young people leaving the care system. The scheme aims to create 10,000 work opportunities over the next 10 years to help young people gain vital skills and experiences as they enter the jobs market: https://mycovenant. org.uk/

- The **Care Experienced Employability Programme** (CEEP) is a one-year pilot programme to help 270 young care leavers aged 16–29 to move into appropriate work, training or educational opportunities. CEEP is led by the Young Person's Consortium (YPC), which consists of Barnardo's Scotland, Action for Children and the Prince's Trust: https://bit.ly/2FQG4wM

- The **Children's Commissioner in Wales** has launched the *Hidden Ambitions* report (https://bit.ly/2n14yH7), which highlights how not all young people leaving foster or residential care get a chance to fulfil their ambitions. On the positive side, she has spoken of good examples of help given by local authorities, and plans to increase opportunities in education, training and other support services: www.childcomwales.org.uk/publications/hidden-ambitions/

- In England, care leavers who choose to start an apprenticeship will receive a £1,000 bursary to help the transition into the workplace. The extra financial support will be for those aged 16–24 and aims to help them in the first year of their apprenticeship as learners transition into the workplace for their practical studies: https://bit.ly/2rOJN5z

Specialist leaving care organisations

These are a few examples of the voluntary sector organisations that provide practical support and training opportunities for care experienced young people.

- **Coram Voice** (including A National Voice) provides specialist advocacy services for care leavers and has a helpline: 0908 800 5792, https://coramvoice.org.uk/professional-zone/care-leavers

- The **Prince's Trust** offers a range of information and schemes to help care leavers into employment: (https://bit.ly/211bw05) and its Fairbridge scheme – which covers all of the UK – offers exciting opportunities for 16–25-year-olds to learn new skills and train: https://bit.ly/2VuCFIM

- In London, the **Drive Forward Foundation** works closely with employers and local authorities to provide specialist support, training and career opportunities for care leavers: www.driveforwardfoundation.com/momentum-made-by-you

You can find details of many other voluntary and statutory organisations online.

How you can help

- Encourage the young person to be ambitious about gaining educational qualifications. It may be that no one from their family has had this opportunity, but that does not mean that the young person should not strive to attain this for himself or herself.

- Don't try to influence the young person's choices but help them think through ideas and get professional help from careers advisers.

- Go with the young person to open days at universities or colleges to help provide them with support.

- Help the young person think through the questions they want to ask about any training or apprenticeships they are considering.

When it's time to move on

I wanted my own place but it helps that my foster carers stay in touch, and I can go there for meals and times like birthdays and stuff.

(Zak, care leaver)

The young person's PA or social worker should help them prepare for the transition to living alone, but you also have a valuable role to play in helping them settle into a new place.

- Help them prepare a list of everything they will need for their new home, whether it's student accommodation or their own flat, or moving in with a partner or friend.

- Encourage them to get involved in local activities – maybe make a list of events on the website MeetUp or give them details of events at the local sports centre, cycling group, drama group, etc.

- If possible, help the young person to move from your home to their new place.

- Stay in regular contact and arrange to visit them if possible.

- Check that the young person is receiving help from appropriate agencies. You will want to encourage them to be as independent as possible, but there are times when we all like to be looked after and the occasional offer of sorting something out for them will be appreciated.

Further resources

Fursland E with Cairns K and Stanway C (2013) *Ten Top Tips for Supporting Education*, London: BAAF

The *Control Freak* series contains three novels that trace the stories of young people in care and leaving care; they can be helpful to young people thinking about what it will be like to leave care.

Bond H (2010) *Control Freak*, London: BAAF

Bond H (2012) *Losing Control*, London: BAAF

Bond H (2013) *Remote Control*, London: BAAF

National Network for the Education of Care Leavers
www.nnecl.org/resources?topic=guides-and-toolkits (England only)

Who Cares? Scotland
www.whocaresscotland.org/who-we-are/blog/how-to-improve-access-to-higher-education/

Become, a charity for young people in care in England, provides information about higher and further education, including Factsheet 4, Helping you Reach Higher, which can be downloaded for free from their website. www.becomecharity.org.uk/for-young-people/care-factsheets/

The **Fostering Network** has a range of resources about education and FE, including the *Toolkit for Schools*.
https://bit.ly/2Tfnp0G

9 Support for foster carers

As has been said before in this guide, fostering teenagers is a challenging task and it is about maintaining a balance between the optimism of knowing that change *can* take place, and being realistic about recognising that you have limits to your own energy and perseverance. If you find that you are no longer able to promote a sense of hope, or help the young person to find resilience after a difficult patch, or that you are no longer committed to holding firm boundaries for the young person, then it is possible that you are reaching burn-out. If you haven't already looked for help from your supporting social worker, this is the time to have a discussion with them.

> *I've had very challenging young people in my home and sometimes I feel nothing is working. Then a young person gets into university and makes a success of their studies and I get such a boost from knowing I achieved that. But without support from my sister, it would've been hard to get him there – and keep myself going.*
>
> (Kala, foster carer)

Recognising your own needs

People choose to foster for a variety of reasons and it is important to ensure that your personal needs are being met, as well as you being able to meet the needs of the young person. Unless it is a two-way process, you are putting yourself at risk of burn-out, which is not good for your physical and/or mental health or that of the young person.

These are questions you may need to ask yourself:

- How satisfied do you feel about what you are achieving?
- Who is it important to get recognition from?

- With whom can you discuss and share what you are going through?

- Can you recognise "compassion fatigue" (https://phys.org/tags/compassion+fatigue/) for yourself and your family?

Writing in *Parenting a Child who has Experienced Trauma*, (2016, pp32–33), Dan Hughes explains that, as foster carers, you need to protect your readiness to maintain care in what may be difficult circumstances.

He suggests that carers need to think about the following areas:

- Remember that providing care is a marathon, not a sprint.

- Caring for yourself so that you are able to consistently care for your child begins with having someone (or some two) to care for you when you need it.

- What are your sources of satisfaction, peace and joy, apart from your identity as a parent and partner?

- Remember that you will make mistakes. You are not a robot or a saint: accept them and learn from them.

- Reflect on your strengths and the challenges that you have overcome as a parent.

- Remember that there is no way of knowing whether even the most difficult situation is hopeless. Many times, after months and even years of very challenging behaviour, a child, teenager, or young adult finally emerges into a life of satisfaction and success.

Helping yourself

Experienced foster carers say that they find it helpful to be very aware of their own need to manage their emotions, learn ways to relax and look after their own stress levels. They also talk about benefitting from having time to switch off from the demands of fostering and pursue their own hobbies and interests. If you don't already have hobbies and ways to relax, then it's very important to find out about what's on offer in your local area.

I have maintained my swimming and walking, my sewing. Whether your thing is Pilates or yoga, or painting or gardening, you need to practise good self-care. And it's no good leaving it until things get really bad, you need to incorporate it into your existence as a foster carer. When things were really bad with my young people, I'd go walking every day, just be in the moment with the amazing sunset and the fabulous trees. Also do things with the young people which take you both away from the emotional side of stuff. I'd take one of my girls out dancing...which we both love. There are places you can go with someone under 18 and family festivals are fantastic. There's not many opportunities for the difficult behaviour to come out...I've met quite a lot of foster carers at WOMAD [music festival].

(Sian, experienced foster carer)

Secondary trauma

It is not unusual for carers of highly traumatised young people to experience secondary trauma. *No One Told Us it was Going to be Like This* was the first national study of compassion fatigue in foster carers in England (https:// phys.org/tags/compassion+fatigue/) and called for greater support and understanding of the effects of caring for some of the most vulnerable children in society. It concluded:

Compassion fatigue is experienced as a physical and emotional response to the stress of caring for those who have experienced trauma. It involves a decrease in empathy and a decline in feelings of pleasure, alongside an increase in stress, anxiety, sleeplessness and negativity. Unlike other people working in helping professions who can go home to rest and escape from a stressful day, a foster carer's home is also their place of work. The study found that without appropriate support to regularly have some "time-out", foster carers are likely to have increased symptoms of compassion fatigue.

(https://bit.ly/2MCi1CC)

The book *Attachment, Trauma and Resilience* (Cairns and Cairns, 2016), also describes looking after traumatised children, and how this can result in compassion fatigue or secondary trauma in carers.

Some fostering placements are easier than others, and some much more challenging. As a carer of very traumatised young people, you might feel that you need therapy. Whether your fostering agency will pay for this is something you will only find out by asking!

Getting support from your supervising social worker

Sometimes carers feel that if they ask for help from their supervising social worker they are admitting that they cannot manage the task. But each young person is different, and you will have your own strengths and weaknesses. Some young people will "push buttons" for you and remind you of past problems. Rather than risk the placement disrupting, be clear in asking for what you need.

Your supervising social worker is there to support you. However, this does not mean that you should go to meetings with them prepared to "dump" all your problems on them. A more positive and constructive approach from you can be helpful in getting what you need. Not only does it save time, but it also helps your worker to realise that you are keen to find a way through the situation.

Take time to prepare for your session. Think through any difficulties you or your family are experiencing, decide what key points you need to make, and also think about some of the solutions that could work for you. In this way, you can go to the meeting feeling resourceful and focused and your social worker is more likely to respond. Demonstrate that you have done your "homework" and looked up information online about approaches, therapies or training that might help you or the young person. Don't expect that you will necessarily get everything you ask for, but if you have a range of options in mind, then you stand a better chance of getting some of these.

If your supervising social worker or the young person's worker simply tells you that you are doing a great job, but you know that you are coming close to breaking point, make this very clear to them. Explain very calmly, using evidence, how this placement is affecting you or your family and that you will need help in order to keep it going.

Being curious is central to caring. If everything feels predictable and if you've tried everything and nothing works, then it is time to ask yourself if you need a break or whether this young person would be better off in another placement. You cannot give a young person what they need if you have no sense of hope or positivity about their future.

Your own children

Studies have shown that placements are more likely to break down if children already in the family are not supportive of them. Fostering is something that is done by the whole family and when you are assessed for fostering, your social worker will want to talk with your children to check that they are supportive of your plans.

Children and young people whose families foster can get many benefits from the experience – such as new friends, learning about empathy for other people's experiences, a sense of responsibility and achievement. Most sons and daughters state that they are happy being part of a fostering family and recognise the benefits of the experience. There is evidence that a proportion of sons and daughters go on to become foster carers themselves or enter the caring professions, and many feel that fostering enhances their social understanding, empathy and skills. In one survey, for example, one-third of children in foster families said that they thought they would become foster carers when they were adults (Fostering Network, 2008). In a review of 14 studies involving the sons and daughters of foster carers, every study showed that fostering had some positive impact on their lives (Fostering Network, 2008).

However, children have also reported that at times they can find it difficult to share their parents and their homes with fostered young people. The behaviour of some young people in the house may make it difficult for them to invite their friends around, or they may be upset by having their privacy invaded and their possessions damaged or stolen. They may find themselves in difficult situations, such as having angry birth parents turn up when their own parents are not at home, or being accused of abuse by foster children. There may also be a sense of unfairness if the fostered young person is given more leeway. They may also find it upsetting when fostered young people whom they have treated as brothers and sisters move on. There's also the possibility that a fostered teenager may introduce your children to cigarettes, alcohol, online games and other things you'd rather they didn't come across, which can add pressures to family relationships.

Studies also show that children in the family may feel that it's difficult for them to make their concerns known or that their parents have not taken their concerns seriously. It's important to create an environment where your own children feel that they are included in decisions, their emotional needs are taken seriously and their opinions valued. If you have any concerns about their well-being, don't overlook these because you are too busy dealing with the more obvious needs of a fostered young person!

Support from peers, friends and family

Support from other foster carers can be extremely beneficial, and fostering services run foster carer support groups which can be beneficial for offloading problems, making useful links, sharing advice, problems and empathy. Some services also run mentoring schemes where very experienced foster carers offer support to other carers. Even if you have a lot of experience yourself, it can be helpful to hear how someone else might approach a situation, or it can be useful simply to talk to someone who has been through similar experiences and can empathise or offer reassurance that there is always a way through.

Having someone in your network who can offer you support is also very important. While support from partners and close friends is vital, having a more neutral person available can also be helpful, as they may be able to see things from a different perspective. You may need to discuss with your supervising social worker how much information you can share with this person.

Respite

Sometimes you just need to take yourself out of a situation for a short while. In some services, foster carers have an entitlement to a certain number of days of respite (when the young person you are fostering stays for a day or two with another carer, in order to give you a break), but this may not always be helpful if a challenging young person has to leave the home. Instead, it may be better to try and arrange for the young person to stay with another foster carer whom they already know, so that this feels more like going to stay at the home of a family friend. Some services also require foster carers to have a back-up carer who can give support when you cannot be around. This person is assessed by your service for this role. Talk to your supervising social worker about the options for delegating authority and young people staying or being cared for by family and friends.

A final word...

The following amusingly and perceptively written book has helped many parents recognise that they are doing a good job under difficult circumstances, and could be a great resource if you're feeling despondent about your ability to understand teenagers.

Franks S and Wolf T (2011) *Get Out of my Life...But First Take me and Alex into Town: The bestselling parents' guide to the new teenager,* London: Profile Books

Bibliography

Adams P (2012) *Planning for Contact in Permanent Placements*, London: BAAF

Aldgate J, Maluccio A and Reeves C (1989) *Adolescents in Foster Families*, London: Lyceum

Bomber LM (2009) 'Survival of the "fittest": teenagers finding their way through the labyrinth of transitions in schools', in Perry A (ed), *Teenagers and Attachment*, London: Worth Publishing

Bomber LM (2016) *Attachment Aware School Series* (box set of five pocket books), London: Worth Publishing

Bond H (2016) *Thinking about Fostering? The definitive guide to fostering in the UK*, London: CoramBAAF

Bowden T and Bowden S (2013) *I just get so...Angry! Dealing with anger and other strong emotions for teenagers*, Wollombi, Australia: Exisle Publishing

Brisch KH (2009) 'Attachment and adolescence', in Perry A (ed) *Teenagers and Attachment*, London: Worth Publishing

Cairns K and Stanway C (2013) *Learn the Child: Helping looked after children to learn*, London: BAAF

Carter P (2013) *Parenting a Child with Autism Spectrum Disorder*, London: BAAF

Coleman J (2016) *Teenagers in Foster Care: A handbook for foster carers and those that support them*, University of Oxford, available online at: https://bit.ly/2kho293

Degamo J (2013) *The Foster Parenting Manual: A practical guide to creating a loving, safe and stable home*, London: Jessica Kingsley Publishers

Degamo J (2014) *Keeping Foster Children Safe Online: Positive strategies to prevent cyberbullying, inappropriate contact, and other digital dangers*, London: Jessica Kingsley Publishers

Davidson R (2006) *Getting Sorted*, London: BAAF

Davidson R (2006) *Getting More Sorted*, London: BAAF

Dubbery C (2015) *Guns, Gangs and the Implications for Social Workers*, London: New Generation

Eagleman D (2015) *The Brain: The story of you*, London: Canongate

Fostering Network (2008) *Fostering Families: Supporting sons and daughters of foster carers*, available online at: https://bit.ly/2Elqhkw

Franks S and Wolf T (2011) *Get Out of my Life...But First Take me and Alex into Town: The bestselling parents' guide to the new teenager*, London: Profile

Fursland (2011) *Foster Care and Social Networking: A guide for social workers and foster carers*, London: BAAF

Fursland E (2016) *The Adopter's Handbook on Therapy*, London: CoramBAAF

Fursland E (2017) *Caring for a Child who has been Sexually Exploited*, London: CoramBAAF

Fursland E (2018) *The Adopter's Handbook on Education*, London: CoramBAAF

Fursland E with Cairns K and Stanway C (2013) *Ten Top Tips for Supporting Education*, London: BAAF

Greenwood L (ed) (2006) *Violent Adolescents: Understanding the destructive impulse*, London: Karnac

Hipgrave T (1989) 'Concepts of parenting and adolescence: implications for fostering adolescents', in Aldgate J, Maluccio A and Reeves C (eds) *Adolescents in Foster Families*, London: Lyceum

Hughes D (2012) *Parenting a Child with Emotional and Behavioural Difficulties*, London: BAAF

Hughes D (2016) *Parenting a Child who has experienced Trauma*, London: CoramBAAF

Jacobs B and Miles L (2012) *Parenting a Child with Attention Deficit Hyperactivity Disorder*, London: BAAF

Jackson S (ed) (2013) *Pathways through Education for Young People in Care: Ideas from research and practice*, London: BAAF

Joughin C and Morley D (2007) *Conduct Disorder in Older Children and Young People: Research messages for practice problems*, London: Research in Practice

Keck GC (2009) *Parenting Adopted Adolescents: Understanding and appreciating their journey*, Colorado Springs, CO: NavPress

Mather M (2018) *Dealing with Foetal Alcohol Spectrum Disorder: A guide for social workers,* London: CoramBAAF

North J (2014) *Mindful Therapeutic Care for Children: A guide to reflective practice*, London: Jessica Kingsley Publishers

Perry A (ed) (2009) *Teenagers and Attachment: Helping adolescents engage with life and learning,* London: Worth Publishing

Plummer DM (2010) *Helping Children Cope with Change, Stress and Anxiety: A photocopiable activities book*, London: Jessica Kingsley Publishers

Quarmby T (2014) 'Sport and physical activity in the lives of looked after children: a "hidden group" in research, policy and practice', *Sport, Education and Society*, 19:7, pp944–958

Schofield G and Beek M (2015) *Promoting Attachment and Resilience: A guide for foster carers and adopters on using the Secure Base model*, London: BAAF

Schofield G and Beek M (2018) *The Attachment Handbook for Foster Care and Adoption* (2nd edn), London: CoramBAAF

Siegel D (2014) *Brainstorm: The power and purpose of the teenage brain*, London: Scribe

Silva RR (2004) *Post Traumatic Stress Disorder in Children and Adolescents: Handbook*, New York, NY: WW Norton

Staff R (2016) *Parenting Adopted Teenagers: Advice for the adolescent years*, London: Jessica Kingsley Publishers

Sunderland M (2012) *Helping Teenagers with Anger and Low Self-Esteem*, Banbury: Hinton House

Taylor C (2010) *A Practical Guide to Caring for Children and Teenagers with Attachment Difficulties*, London: Jessica Kingsley Publishers

Warwick P and Whitehouse E (2014) *Adolescent Volcanoes: Helping adolescents and their parents to deal with anger*, London: Jessica Kingsley Publishers

Youell B (2016) *Parenting a Child Affected by Sexual Abuse*, London: CoramBAAF

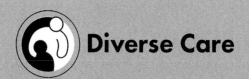 **Diverse Care**

Could fostering be your cup of tea?

Drop us a call on:
0800-7-747-747
Or register your interest online at
www.diversecare.com

Do something amazing... become a Foster Parent.

Could you help to put a teenager on the right road to a bright future?

FOSTER CARERS ARE NEEDED NOW IN THE NORTH EAST AND NORTH WEST OF ENGLAND

Foster Cares Ltd. is an independent fostering agency covering the North of England with offices in Durham and Warrington

To find out more
call Freephone 0800 488 0081

or call one of our offices:

North East
0191 586 9655

North West
0161 872 7048

FOSTER CARES
LIMITED

Be brave, be brilliant, be a foster carer

Call 0800 05 222 50

or email referrals@togethertrust.org.uk

together trust

Registered charity number 209782

Have you ever thought of fostering?

Make a difference... foster for us

Whether it's full time or weekend fostering that you're thinking about, Tree House needs carers for both!

Do you want to:

🖐 Join a professional team who want to do the right thing for every child

🖐 Have a high level of support provided by an experienced fostering social worker

🖐 Receive outstanding training and a generous allowance for each child

Contact us today:

If you want to join us and do something really wonderful we'd love to hear from you

Freephone: **0800 012 6507**

Email: **fostering@treehousecare.org**

Website: **www.treehousecare.org**

f facebook.com/Treehousecarefostering

🐦 twitter.com/TreeHouseCare

We are recruiting carers in:
Lincolnshire & Humberside,
Yorkshire & East Midlands
and across the North West

Tree House Care
doing the right thing for our children

Head Office :
Tree House Care
17 Heneage Road, Grimsby
N. E. Lincolnshire, DN32 9DZ